GROWING UP IRISH

Adventures with the Team That Shaped My Life
True stories of family, friends and football

by Mark Andrew Hamer

Best wishes

Mark Andrew Hamer

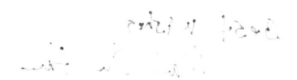

Table of Contents

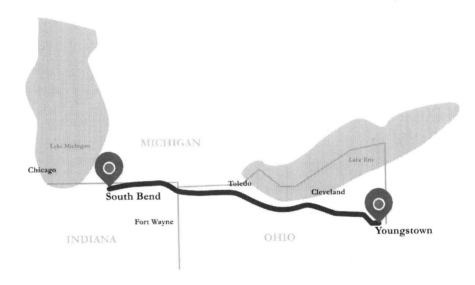

4 h 49 min
314 miles

Preface

Family is something you are born into. You have no control over who your mother, father, brothers, or sisters are. Some are more fortunate than others to be born into supportive, nurturing families with parents and siblings who help guide and develop you into who you are as a person. I am one of those fortunate people. I was born into a Notre Dame family. I'd like to say I had a choice in my collegiate allegiance, but in reality, I didn't. I was molded and shaped into an Irish diehard through years of exposure to the institution through annual pilgrimages to football games. I wouldn't say I was brainwashed, but maybe the word *trained* is more appropriate. I became a product of my environment—an environment that revolved around true dedication to the gold and blue.

Not only did I become a Notre Dame fanatic, but I also became closer to my father. It was my father who started the Notre Dame traditions in our family. It was my father who took his five children to football games, rallies, and Irish events. Through the many trips to South Bend, Indiana, I had the opportunity to spend quality father and son time with my dad. I got to learn better who he is as a person, more so than I could have in the course of typical everyday interactions.

Those experiences inspired me to write this book. I want to preserve the memories from those annual trips with Dad. They were special times full of camaraderie and life lessons. Lessons I would like to pass down to my own children in my own way. I will try my best to groom them to be Notre Dame homers, but ultimately, it's up to them. Regardless of their level of commitment, I want them to still have the opportunity to learn the same life lessons I did. I want them to be able to hear the stories and get to know my father the way I did. I want them to get to know the institution that brought us all together as a family. My hope is that you, the reader, will gain a stronger sense of family and take the opportunity to share the significant experiences in your own life with your loved ones. Quality time is fleeting, and I want to inspire an appreciation for time spent with the people who are most important in life.

Growing up, Notre Dame University was the catalyst for our family unity, and it remains the constant that brings us all together. This book is a collection of stories, accompanied by some NDU history, that describes some of my favorite experiences and life lessons that resulted from those annual trips to South Bend. In essence, this is a lifetime story in the making.

Chapter 1
The Note

The early morning air was crisp in northern Ohio as I walked to school. The autumn leaves covered the ground and crunched under my solid black uniform shoes. Eager to get there, I ran ahead of my older siblings who were walking slowly, taking their time. Maybe they just weren't filled with the same excitement as I was to get to school that day. I reached the five-lane road separating my street from the school. I stopped and yelled to my siblings, "Rob, Laura, Katie, hurry up!" My voice carried sharply, visibly rising as a pale white steam in the cold air. For some reason the usually punctual crossing guard was absent, and I was getting impatient waiting there at the stop light. I wanted to leave my brother and sisters behind and just run to school, but my mother's words in my head reminded me that I was forbidden to cross this road without holding a hand, ever.

After my siblings finally caught up, we crossed the road and walked past St. Charles Church. It was the largest church in town. Its steeple was built to be the highest point in the county and could be seen for miles. Our school building, on the other hand, was the smaller structure that sat in the shadow of that grand cathedral. My siblings and I parted ways at the door of the school. While they headed to the upper grade classrooms on the second floor, I took the stairs down to the first floor where the younger students were. I put my hat (dark blue with a gold block Notre Dame logo) in my wooden locker and took a seat at my creaky desk. The sounds of children's chatter filled the room as we waited for the teacher to start morning prayers. The green chalkboard at the front of the room was clean from the day before. One lucky student had been selected for board duty, taking a bucket of cold water and a sponge and wiping the chalk-covered slate clean with surgical precision. Each vertical swipe of the sponge had left behind perfectly straight lines of slightly opaque chalk residue, creating a green and white striped pattern across the board.

To my first-grade eyes it no longer resembled a chalkboard. All I could see was a football field. I silently counted out yard line markers on each of the chalk stripes . . . *10, 20, 30, 40, 50, 40, 30, 20, 10, end zone.* I imagined myself running down the sidelines, returning a kick for a score. I was no longer in Mrs. Friedman's first grade classroom wearing my Catholic school-approved solid navy pants and a solid white collared shirt. In my mind I was wearing a blue and gold football uniform with a gold-plated helmet shining in the sun. I was proudly standing in the end zone of Notre Dame stadium with thousands of fans cheering my name. The number 25 on my chest might as well have been a Superman logo, given the crowd's electrifying response.

Then the school bell rang loudly and my all-too-perfect daydream was interrupted by my teacher officially starting the school day with the words "Our father, who art in heaven . . ." All the students joined in to recite the morning prayers. After an "Our Father" and "Hail Mary," the teacher asked if there was anything special anyone wanted to pray for. I felt the excitement return to my core as my hand instantly shot up in the air.

"Yes, Mark?" the teachers asked.

Without hesitation I blurted out: "Please pray for me to have a safe trip to Notre Dame Stadium."

You see, that day was a special day. There was a reason I was so excited to get to school. At dinner the night before, my father had told me I was finally old enough to go with him and the ND crew to a Notre Dame football game. This was a huge deal in my family. It was the rite of passage I had been waiting for my entire seven-year life. I couldn't wait to get to school to tell all my friends. What better way to announce the big news than with prayer?

As I look back at my first-grade self I can only laugh. You see, it was October when my father told me I could go to the spring football game . . . in April. Although my big announcement was somewhat premature, like the movie *Groundhog Day*, I repeated that morning petition routine for six months. I can only imagine how tired everyone must have been of hearing it. But God bless her heart, Mrs. Friedman, let me petition a blessing every morning for six straight months. It's a good thing, too, because whether it was morning prayer time, lunchtime, or any other time, I was going to announce my trip to the Notre Dame spring game every day until we set off for the stadium. I reasoned that at least getting it out of the way early during morning prayers allowed everyone to move on with the day.

❉❉❉

The Notre Dame spring football game, more commonly known as the Blue-Gold game, is the annual University of Notre Dame scrimmage. It's an opportunity for fans and coaches to get a sneak peek at the Fighting Irish football squad for the upcoming fall season. The game has been played each spring for almost ninety years. The players have the opportunity to state their case for a starting position while the fans can get an insider look at the organization.

The trip to Notre Dame each spring was a huge deal in my family. Looking back, I realize it was more than just a football game. It was a time to reconnect with family and friends. We were always accompanied by my father's best pals on the trek across I-80 west to the promised land. For me, most of the excitement stemmed from having the opportunity for a weekend adventure with my father. My mother would stay home taking care of the endless duties that come with having five children. Those who were old enough would pack up and hit the road to spend some quality time with Dad while I'm sure Mom got some much-deserved peace and quiet at home. The drive itself was part of the experience too. A four-hour drive with a caravan of cars full of children can easily turn into five, six, or even seven hours. The patience our dads must have had on these annual fathers-only trips must have been mammoth. A weekend looking out for that many children without the support and guidance of Mom would be a real challenge for any father.

We would officially hit the road early on a Friday morning and would return late afternoon that Sunday. It was only a two-day trip, but I remember packing as if we would be gone for weeks on a safari to a foreign land. We would load the car on Thursday night with bags, suitcases, coolers, and food. Packing the family vehicle was a complex game of Tetris that my father had mastered. I don't know how everything fit with five children—especially when each of us brought two bags, pillows, and, most importantly, football gear. Children do not travel light.

In order to miss a day of school on purpose, a very special note from a parent needed to go to the principal of the school for the absence to be approved. My saint of a mother would write us all notes to take into school the Thursday before we were leaving. That simple piece of paper would liberate us from the obligation of perfect attendance.

My child (Rob, Laura, Katie, Mark, or David), will not be in school Friday. They will be going on a family trip with their father to visit the campus of Notre Dame University in South Bend, Indiana. Please excuse their absence. I will be sure to work extra hard to help them make up any work they may miss. Thank you, God bless. —Janet

The all-important note. Without that note, the trip wouldn't be possible. I treated it like gold. It never left my sight from the time my mother put it in my book bag on Thursday morning to the time I got to class. During the short, one-mile walk to school, I must have checked about a thousand times to make sure it was still in my bag—as if some note-stealing monster would sneak up while I wasn't looking and snatch it away. Or magically a gust of wind would find its way into my bag and snag the note from the clutches of the ten-pound math book that was meant to safeguard it. If that note got lost, all my hopes and dreams would be lost with it. What a terribly heavy burden for a child to bear, right?

I remember the sense of massive relief I felt after I handed the note to my teacher. I ran straight up to her and hand delivered it. To leave no doubt, I asked her to read it right then and there. It was the most important task of the day, the mission of all missions. Until she read the words that blessed that blue-lined paper, my soul could not rest. My nerves got the best of me that morning; sweat beaded and ran down my face and my lungs went into overdrive, resulting in monstrous breathing. It was a very emotionally and physically taxing experience. My teacher kindly complied with my urgent request when I handed her the note. As I looked up at her reading the words, the massive weight on my shoulders was lifted to the heavens. It was a glorious moment. *Ah, it's out of my hands now,* I thought. *Onward to victory.*

Chapter 2
The Horsemen

S team rises over fresh poured coffee at a table for three. It's 10:00 a.m. on the third Tuesday of the month. People come and go with their McDonald's breakfast orders, but my father and his two best friends sit there chatting away. Howard and Big Al, as they are affectionately referred to, are lifelong friends of our family. This traditional monthly meetup is a way for the three of them to keep up with what is going on in their ever-changing lives. They are all retired—well, technically Howard isn't. He still goes into the office every now and then to stay busy. This colloquial trio is a treasure trove of knowledge, eager to share lifetimes of stories and memories. Memories of how they all first met at a recreational basketball league at St. Charles Church, or how they all volunteered to work the beer booth every summer for the church festival. (If I remember right, they called themselves the Booze Brothers. Clever name, right?) They even volunteered together to help work the Sunday pancake breakfast after Mass at our parish social hall.

You might see the pattern here. Church activities played a big part in my life growing up. That is where we prayed, socialized, and made friends. I grew an appreciation for that church, constantly being immersed in a crowd of like-minded individuals. I learned how to meet new people and always be respectful, ideals strengthened by the example my parents set. The location of that church played a key role in our participation since it was only a block from my childhood home. Ironically, the McDonald's that my father, Howard, and Big Al frequent is adjacent to that reverent religious rendezvous. The three discuss Notre Dame football, complain about things, discuss Notre Dame football again, then find something else to complain about. Topics vary; sometimes it's politics, sometimes government, sometimes children and grandchildren, but they always come back to Notre Dame football. It's the glue that holds their forty-year relationship together.

I have literally known Howard and Big Al my entire life. They are like family. Growing up, whenever there was a barbecue, graduation party, or even a wedding, those guys were first on the invite list. They are great friends of my parents and have been like pseudo dads to us kids. Howard was a financial advisor and father of three. Al was a postman and father of two. My father, who they call "Caner," (more about that in chapter 5) was a steel worker and father of five. Together we all made up the Notre Dame clan. Over the years others came and went, but these three remained the patriarchal band of brothers that led our group to South Bend every year. They are unequivocally the source of my deep-rooted connection to the blue and gold, the doctrine that bridges my adult life to my youth.

Drawing parallels between my life and Notre Dame lore is like a complex game of connect the dots. The resulting image can be an abstract illusion or a crystal-clear depiction of veracity. The latter is the case when I look at my father and his pals and how their devotion to the Irish shaped my reality. There are similar stories throughout history where a select few have influenced the trajectory of others by unintentionally leading them on a path to destiny with simple actions. When I see my father and his pals together, leading us onward to victory (and by "victory" I mean South Bend, Indiana), I am reminded of a classic Notre Dame football narrative. One that depicts a few young men as the impetus to the path of greatness. I'm talking about the story of the Four Horsemen.

✽✽✽

The Four Horsemen of Notre Dame was a group of young men who played for the Irish under head coach Knute Rockne. Quarterback Harry Stuhldreher, left halfback Jim Crowley, right halfback Don Miller, and fullback Elmer Layden led the team as the offensive backfield from 1922 to 1924. In dramatic fashion, a game played early in the 1924 season served as the catalyst for one of the best publicity campaigns in Notre Dame history.

"The Four Horsemen of Notre Dame" was a nickname penned by sportswriter Grantland Rice of the former *New York Herald Tribune*. On October 18, 1924, the Irish traveled to New York to play a very strong US Army team. Notre Dame came out victorious with a score of 13–7. It was a statement game for the Irish. Today we would call it a "signature win." The performance of Stuhldreher, Crowley, Miller, and Layden had a profound impact on Rice. After the game, he wrote:

> Outlined against a blue-gray October sky, the Four Horsemen rode again. In dramatic lore their names are Death, Destruction, Pestilence, and Famine. But those are aliases. Their real names are: Stuhldreher, Crowley, Miller, and Layden. They formed the crest of the South Bend cyclone before which another fighting Army team was swept over the precipice at the Polo Grounds this afternoon as 55,000 spectators peered down upon the bewildering panorama spread out upon the green plain below.[1]

The story goes that upon returning to South Bend after the game, a student by the name of George Strickler did his part to make the name stick. Inspired by the *New York Herald* article, Strickler rounded up four horses from a stable in town. He posed Stuhldreher, Crowley, Miller, and Layden in full uniform on the backs of the animals and took an iconic photo. Adding the visual to the name was a powerful tool to spike the interest of the public. The photo was printed in almost every newspaper in America, and the legend of the Four Horsemen was born.

"At the time, I didn't realize the impact it would have," Crowley said later. "But the thing just mushroomed. After the splurge in the press, the sports fans of the nation got interested in us along with other sportswriters. Our record helped, too. If we'd lost a couple. I don't think we would have been remembered."[2]

The Irish would go on to be undefeated during that 1924 season, a perfect 10–0 record. A win over Stanford in the Rose Bowl earned them the national title. The Four Horsemen played a total of thirty games together while at Notre Dame. During that time they only lost to one other school, Nebraska. They became iconic treasures of Irish lore. As leaders of the team for three seasons, they were almost perfect. Likewise, when I think of my father and his buddies as the leaders of our family team, I see victories that surpass those of the Four Horsemen. I see my father's band of brothers as, well, perfect. All those years of taking all us children to games and creating fond memories has had a lasting impression on me.

One cold winter morning when I was back in my hometown as a grown man with children of my own, I was invited to their monthly caffeine-fueled powwow. As I sat at the McDonald's table and listened to the three banter and fire away, I felt like I was in a time machine. I heard the same stories I have heard over and over again. It was as if nothing had changed. They were loud and somewhat obnoxious but also friendly and nonthreatening. Some might have found them too obnoxious, but not me. I found the vibrant exchange comforting, a pleasant reminder of my youth. They were a chatty bunch, making new friends through inquisitive conversation with strangers passing by. The same routine they used in South Bend all those years to strike up a dialogue with other like-minded Notre Dame fanatics during game weekends.

Each one of them brought their own unique dynamic to the conversation. Al, the comic relief, with his quick wit and friendly demeanor, is easily approachable. Howard, the all-knowing, can recall places, dates, teams, and any other facts about Notre Dame football, adding legitimacy to the discussion. My father, a man's man, brings street cred and sensibility. Together they make a great team. I learned a lot observing the social interaction of this trio. It was hard not to. They can be a very polarizing group. The way they met new people, the way they organized a trip to be relaxing and fun, the way they used reason and sensibility to make decisions—I soaked it all in like a sponge, unbeknownst to them. They are definitely people to look up to, and I feel privileged having the opportunity to be a part of the group. Seeing how they did things and approached the world was truly educational and helped structure a foundation for being a good person.

However, as I've gotten older, I've noticed some, well, let's just say "chinks in the armor" regarding their social strategies. One example that sticks in my mind is the process it takes to "get tickets." Now most of the time the three of them would acquire tickets well before we left Ohio. Months in advance of a game they would search high and low for the best deals. In fact, we would always pick what game we were going to at the end of the trip the previous year. Tickets sometimes came through friends, ticket brokers, or even the university itself. The point here is they always had tickets.

During game weekends ticket scalpers come out of the woodwork and set up shop on every street corner in town. One of the most notable streets is East Angela Boulevard, right off North Michigan Street. East Angela leads right up to the university and is pretty much the only way to get to the stadium. I am sure there are other ways, but that was the way we always went. This street has more ticket scalpers than any other street. My father, Big Al, and Howard love to play this game of "squabble with a scalper." Normally my father is driving and Al is hanging out the passenger window as we stop at every ticket broker we see to "negotiate." I can recite the routine by heart because the exchange is always the same. Howard first yells from the back seat, "What is this guy asking for tickets?" Then my father pulls over, and Al says two words to the scalper: "How much?"

Now the scalper (who is normally friendly at first, because he is trying to make a sale) will be a little inquisitive and ask what kind of seats we want.

With no further direction or clarification from anyone, my dad will just yell from the driver seat again, "How much?"

Not quite annoyed yet, the scalper will reply, "Well, I don't know where you want to sit, but I have these tickets for, (enter any price here)."

Then, in unison, my father, Big Al, and Howard all throw their hands in the air in disgust, implying the price is outrageous and there is no way they will spend that much.

The scalper (now on the brink of frustration) will reply, "Well, how much are you willing to spend?"

Al will give an insultingly low number that will infuriate the scalper as my dad hits the gas and we move on.

Now imagine doing this routine with every scalper on the street. East Angela is not a long road, so scalpers could be just a few hundred feet apart. They would repeat the charade over and over, knowing full well they had plenty of perfectly good tickets in hand already.

Now keep imagining us sitting in backed up traffic as the scalper we just insulted walks past the car again, giving the all-too-familiar evil eye. I can't put into words how much the trio loves doing this act. They pretend they are mad, and then they crack up as we pull away. As a child, I too thought it was hilarious, but then around the age of thirteen, I started to get embarrassed. Maybe I just hit the age where everything your parents do is embarrassing, or maybe I was just wise beyond my years. Who knows. I just know it was a routine that made them happy. Nobody got hurt, and they got a laugh. After all, that is what our trips to South Bend were all about anyway. To have fun and enjoy time with friends. I will say though that because of this charade, I did learn how to get the best ticket price. But as my father gets older and I inevitably take on the role of the team bus driver, when we have tickets in hand, I am not stopping the vehicle. I can happily go without playing squabble with the scalpers. My father and his friends have started the traditions here; I just look at it as putting my own spin on a classic game by keeping my foot on the gas.

Chapter 3
Turning Points

P art of the allure of Notre Dame football for a child fan is having the opportunity to see something magical, to witness something special, and even better yet—to be part of something great. That was what the spring game was for me. The university opened its doors showing a little of what was behind the gridiron curtain. As loyal fans we had the opportunity to take a deeper dive into the football program. Before the spring scrimmage, we could walk out on the field, meet the players, and even tour the practice facilities. As a child who grew up playing football myself, this was transformational. It was a way to see how the "big kids" did it. To be forthright, it was one of those experiences that really fueled my love for the game and inspired me to stick with it as long as I could.

Football became a part of me. Not because my father loved it or my brother loved it or friends loved it but because I loved it. Having next-level access to the sport really helped me develop passion for the game by cultivating the discovery of what made me happy. I was lucky to have that opportunity. Wouldn't it be great if every child could have access at an early age to professional disciplines that inspired them? As a society, we do our best to educate and inspire our children with the hope they find their own individual path to a fulfilling life. But that kind of cerebral nourishment is not as ubiquitous as it should be. I hear all the time that programs are being dropped from schools. Programs like music and art are being left behind in some parts of the country. Those are the programs that evoke drive and passion in developing children. If they are not exposed to programs like that early on, how can they ever discover where their true passions are? I feel fortunate to have had those kinds of stimulating experiences growing up. Experiences like the ones I had on my trips to Notre Dame with my family provoked curiosity and excitement for something. They helped me discover a simple truth . . . I love the game of football.

I can trace the genesis of that truth all the way back to one moment in my life. It happened right outside the Notre Dame indoor practice facility when I was eight years old. It was right before the annual spring game, the blue against the gold. They don't do this anymore, but at the time, the university allowed fans to go through the practice and training facilities. I remember standing outside the locker-room door with my father—and many other Irish followers. We were watching the players come out before they made their way to the field to start the game. I stood there in the front row with hundreds of other eight-year-old kids. We made a basic receiving line and gave high fives to the players as they walked by. I knew most of the players but a few I didn't.

There was a new player who walked out the door. He must have been a true freshmen because I didn't know anything about him. He wore number 87 that day. As he walked by, I reached out my hand for a high five, and with a smile, he handed me a fresh player towel. It was the kind wide receivers wear. It had Velcro on the top so it could be secured to a belt during play. It was white with the ND logo on the top. It was brand new, and it was mine. My first piece of official Notre Game player gear. I was so excited—what a moment! Here I was, an ordinary eight-year-old kid among hundreds of other ordinary eight-year-old kids, and number 87 picked me.

Up until that point, my main reason for wanting to go to Notre Dame was to spend time with Dad, but something changed within me at that very moment. Don't get me wrong—I still was excited about being there with my father, but now I had another reason. That was the moment I became a true Notre Dame diehard. It was transformational, and dare I say, magical. I knew right then that I wanted to play football too. A few months later, I asked my parents if they could sign me up to play, and with no hesitation they agreed.

That moment outside the locker room was a turning point for me. It seems trite, but I can recall how it actually launched my enthusiasm for the sport. I took that towel with me that day and wore it for all my football games all the way through high school. It's funny how the smallest things can have the biggest impact on people in totally unexpected ways. It's so crazy to think that a simple towel from a player could set me on a path that indirectly affected where I would end up today. I became a student of the game that day and all that it entails. Football teaches hard work, dedication, fortitude, and teamwork. These are lessons that not only make a person successful in the game but successful in life.

I found out later that number 87 was Lake Dawson. He played for the Irish for four years as a wide receiver. He was eventually drafted into the NFL by the Kansas City Chiefs and played a number of years before he retired due to injury. I never spoke to him and never saw him in person again. But that one moment stands out in my mind to this day. Reflecting back on that day when I was eight years old, standing in that hallway wide-eyed and highly impressionable, I realize that inspiration can come from anywhere or anybody. That even the simplest gestures can have huge impacts.

In the years that followed I became motivated to return the favor. Maybe not to Mr. Dawson directly, but to pay him back by being a positive influence on someone else. Call it reciprocity, call it karma, call it what you want, but doesn't it seem true that you get back what you give? Shouldn't we all give back a little so everyone has access to opportunities that may change their lives. We all need a little nudge here and there to experience that magic that helps us learn and grow. For me it was sports, for others it could be music, a poem, a book, or maybe a piece of art. What a special gift it is to help others find their muse or discover their purpose. Being around positively influential people creates positively influential people doesn't it? A wise expert on evaluating potential once said:

> As you go through life you have experiences that teach you things. Wins, losses. I've learned a lot more from my losses than my wins. I've learned how important it is to get the right people in the right places. At the end of the day, the profits come from the type of people you bring in.[1]

I find it very fitting that the man who said that is the same man who gave me that towel.

Chapter 4
Blue Pants and White Shirts

A furiously oscillating hammer struck a bell in my Catholic grade school. The bustling hallway became silent as students flocked to their classrooms. Some of the more patient teachers waited a moment before closing their doors to allow for latecomers and slow movers to make their way to the classroom. In my school, you weren't late until the door shut. That was the cutoff point. If the door was closed, that signaled you needed to go right to the principal's office to get a late slip. Three late slips led to detention, detention led to a grounding at home, and a grounding at home led to missing out on something exciting with your friends. So, of course, nobody wanted to be late. Sure, there were the students who weren't phased by this rule. Maybe they liked detention, or maybe sleeping in was a priority, or maybe they had parents who didn't ground them. I don't know, but there were those who were perpetually tardy.

I was not one of them. Not because I didn't enjoy sleeping in. It was mostly out of fear of my mother. Being late for school was something she couldn't tolerate. She was an early riser and made sure my brothers and sisters and I were too. Despite our best efforts, we could never sleep in, not even on the weekends. Couple that with the fact that we lived only a block from school, and we had no excuse for being late. Plus, we walked most of the time; we couldn't even blame the bus. It was a fact: Hamers were always punctual. I wish I could have parlayed that truth to be a more permanent fixture later in my life. Nowadays I am late for everything, but as a child going to St. Charles Borromeo Catholic School, I never arrived after the morning bell.

Almost never. I remember hearing the bell ring that day from across the street as I was making my way to school. The traffic light was red, keeping me from crossing. I dared not cross without the "walk" sign glowing white, under threat of certain punishment or death. With a helpless feeling I paced back and forth at the corner impatiently, waiting for the light to change. Seconds seemed like hours. The light finally turned green, and like a wild bobcat liberated from a snare, I dashed across the street, up the front steps of the school, through the door, and down the hallway. I was one of the hallway stragglers now, racing to make it to the classroom door before it conclusively slammed shut. Like a prison door locking into place, the sound of that door closing had definitive meaning. It's a sound that still haunts me today. Every time I hear a door close, my mind goes to a place of cold finality.

But I was too late. The door had shut; I had missed it. Like Charlie Brown I hung my head and slowly walked toward the principal's office. *Dead man walking,* I thought. How was my mother going to react to this? Not good. Only by seconds this became my first delinquent day of the year, but I anticipated my mother would skip right to the socially crippling grounding when she got the news of this reprehensible misconduct. As I got closer to the principal's door, I tried to think of good excuses that might free me from the tardy slip of shame. *My dog ate my homework? No, that won't work. I don't have a dog. My sister made me late? No, Katie is more paranoid about being late than me and would never let that happen. I got it: Mrs. Morley, the older lady across the street, needed help bringing in her groceries . . . No. Why would she have groceries at 7:30 a.m. on a Friday?* I was doomed, there was nothing I could do or say to get me out of a certain grounding. That is, there was nothing my fifth-grade mind was willing to admit for cause of this malfeasance, out of fear of certain embarrassment. You see, I did have my reasons for being late that day. But first let me explain something.

It is no secret that uniforms are a must in the Catholic education system. In my school the boys were required to wear a solid blue or white shirt with solid blue or black slacks and black shoes. For girls it was a solid blue or white shirt with a plaid skirt that could hang no higher than an inch above the knee. Uniforms were a blessing and a curse. On one hand they were boring and non-expressive. On the other hand they made life easier. That is to say, you didn't have to really worry about what you were going to wear or put much thought into what everyone else was wearing. Like all rules, the daily dress code had its exceptions. Every once in a while we had a dress-down day. A day that we could break the humdrum of ritual and wear clothing outside the rules of the standard uniform. It was usually on a Friday and usually for a special occasion. It was an exciting, albeit nerve-wracking, ordeal. This just happened to be one of those occasions.

I can't remember why we were granted the dress-down day, I just remember it was an opportunity to break from the norm and actually wear something that, in a way, was a reflection of our personalities. These days came very infrequently, so there was a lot of pressure. Couple that with the fact that I was in fifth grade—the awkward period in life when clothes and appearance really start to matter. I had totally overthought the situation and had a real quandary on my hands. Earlier that morning, looking down at the clothing choices I had laid out on my bed, I stood there perplexed. *Oh, what to do, what to do?* I thought. This decision was huge. It could quite possibly launch my fashion prestige among my peers or send it spiraling down in an inglorious blaze. Glaring at those wardrobe selections, I took forever to make the decision. I pondered and pondered, going over every possible scenario in my head, from what my friends would think to the reaction I would get from that girl I liked. It was very stressful and time-consuming. I had paced around the room in frustration and angst. I was lost. The answer wasn't coming to me. I tried one more time to look upon the choices and ask myself, *Do I go with the blue Notre Dame football T-shirt or the green Notre Dame T-shirt?* Such a difficult decision. I didn't want to screw this up. I wanted to give my classmates the impression that I was both fashion-forward and sporty at the same time. The fifth-grade mind is a complicated thing, constantly exploring uncharted areas and looking at the world as if every decision were a matter of life and death. The process of going through the pros and cons of my T-shirt selection made me lose track of time. Before I knew it, I was late. I went with the blue shirt and ran out the door.

Obviously my developing, obsessive-compulsive fifth-grade mind made a much bigger deal out of dress-down day than was necessary. In all actuality, it should have been an extremely easy decision. At that time in my life I only had three outfits to wear. I had my school uniform, my Sunday Mass clothes, and my ND gear.

I had accumulated a lot of Notre Dame apparel over the years, gifted to me by my father. Before I ever made my first adventure to South Bend, my dad was a seasoned pro. Every year, like clockwork, he would go to a game and every year he would come home with souvenirs for my siblings and I. He would walk through the door on a Sunday afternoon returning from his South Bend voyage holding bags of surprises for us kids. It was such an exciting time. "What did you get us! What did you get us!" we would all scream, crowding the door and barely letting him in. He would always say, "Go sit down, go sit down." We would make our way to the living room couch and impatiently sit as Dad handed out the goods. Sometimes it was a T-shirt, other times a hat—maybe even a football if we were lucky. Always, always it was something labeled with the crosshatched ND logo. We were always so excited to get whatever it was he brought back. I remember sometimes we even got the same T-shirt that we'd gotten the previous year. We didn't care though; it was new and exciting.

For me, when Dad came home with Notre Dame swag, it was more thrilling than my birthday. Partly because we got cool Notre Dame stuff and partly because my dad was home to tell us stories about the game. I was always so fascinated with what the game was like. How many people were there? Did you see any players? Did you get any autographs? So many questions went through my mind that I wanted to ask my father. He would get his coffee, and we would sit and chat about the game. It really didn't matter if it was a win or a loss by that point. It was more about going over the details of the game, like Tony Rice ran for a touchdown or Chris Zorich had a sack. I have such fond memories of those Sundays.

My dad certainly did his part to ensure we grew up as Notre Dame fans. He would give us gifts, and we would talk ND football. I guess, subconsciously, at a young age, we associated talking football with getting stuff. Kind of like how you teach a dog to speak or rollover with a dog treat. Whether we knew it or not we were being groomed to be Irish faithful.

One of my favorite souvenirs was a kid-sized football. The kind that was perfect for the playground at school. One half was blue, one half was gold, and the strings were white. It had a blue ND logo printed on the side. I took that ball everywhere with me. It always had to have a place in my book bag. I would throw it around in the yard, in the house, everywhere. The best was when my dad would play catch with me in the front yard with it. We would pretend we were ND players. He was Steve Beuerlein and I was Tim Brown. Our yard was small, so to go out for a pass I would always have to dodge the maple tree in the neighbor's yard. They didn't mind though. Our yard combined with the neighbor's yard made for the perfect football field. The driveway that separated both lots was the fifty-yard line. We used to play football in the front yard for hours; well into the night sometimes. My mom would turn on the front porch light so we could see.

As children we didn't need much. I was perfectly happy with a football and a T-shirt. In fact, I would have been happy with just the football. We lived a very simple and modest life. My parents are very simple and modest people: church, school, and work with football in between. That was pretty much it. My parents and the five of us children lived happily in a small house. The Catholic ideals of Notre Dame blended perfectly with our family lifestyle. With that in mind, it seems funny that I let the social pressures of wardrobe selection get to me so much on that day that it resulted in a tardy slip. That was the only time I was late that year. In fact, if I really think about it, it was the only time I was late for school ever. Even though I terribly feared the repercussions I would face from my mother, she pleasantly let it slide as long as it didn't happen again. And neither my friends, nor that girl I liked, really paid attention to my blue shirt.

Chapter 5
The Birth of a Hurricane

In 1984, American culture shifted: The first Macintosh computer made its way onto desktops, Discovery rocketed into the heavens, and my father made his first visit to South Bend. Of course Big Al and Howard were there too. This was the first official pilgrimage—the one that launched a legacy. With all the colossal events happening throughout the country, this small one would have the biggest impact on my life directly, although its importance in my life wouldn't be clear for decades. Since I was a small child at the time.

Miami Vice burst into living rooms that year as well and became the most popular show on television with its palm trees, rolled-up blazer sleeves, and bright neon-covered, well, everything. So it is almost poetic that the first Notre Dame game they attended was against the University of Miami. Around this time, the Florida school was just starting its climb to football greatness. They were the new kids on the block, the underdogs, and a real thrill to watch. Notre Dame had been a top-tier team for a while, so finding tickets to the game was challenging. Even though the game was played in South Bend in 1984, my father and company had to use some astute "sleuthiness" to find tickets. Inspired by the detective work on

Miami Vice, Howard took it upon himself to meet the challenge. He failed at his first attempt; Notre Dame was asking outrageous prices. That didn't slow him down. With his clever resolve, he made some calls down to the University of Miami and secured five tickets, but with a catch: At the time, Miami was on the rise and trying to increase its national reach. So in order to get tickets, Howard had to join the University of Miami Athletics Booster Club. Since he was already a Notre Dame diehard, this was tough for him to do. But he swallowed his pride and played the martyr. The tickets arrived, along with a booster welcome package, including some Miami tchotchkes and one obnoxious green and orange hat. Howard planned to stomp on it in the Notre Dame tailgate lot before the game.

When they had made it to South Bend, and it came time for the ceremonial stomping, Howard took out the hat and raised it into the air. The dramatic show he displayed caused a small crowd to form around him. With intoxicated guttural cheers, supportive onlookers showed their approval for the looming apparel defacement. Howard yelled out, "Down with the Canes!" And just as his raised arm started its descent to send the hat slamming to the ground, my father reached out and grabbed Howard's wrist, halting the display. With that contrarian gesture, not only did my father stop Howard's arm at the precipice of provoking pandemonium, but he literally single-handedly silenced a crowd.

"What did you do that for?" Howard asked.

My antagonistic father replied, "I want to see what kind of reaction I get from everyone if I wear it around campus."

With all the befuddled bystanders looking on, my father took the hat and put it on his proud head. Within seconds, insults were flung from every direction, but my father didn't care. To him it was funny, a twisted game of "madden the masses." And it worked, because everywhere he went, it got people fired up, especially in the stadium. How dare he wear orange and green among the blue and gold! He was pelted with insults, but my father just put his hands in the air and smiled.

That seemingly simple antic really rubbed some folks the wrong way. After the game, when the guys walked back to the car, they were surprised to find that a mischievous leprechaun had paid them a visit. He didn't leave green candy or innocent tricks but something a little more permanent. Something more crafty and artistic. That little elf put his creativity to work in the form of a self-portrait keyed into the side of the vehicle. The artwork portrayed the proud Irish figure standing on top of the word "Canes." In a complete role reversal, my father's jubilation magically transformed into exasperation as the rest of the group burst out laughing. His car was tattooed with a florid reminder that this was Irish country.

He would later get that artwork removed, but he could never shake the nickname he earned that day. The guys all called him "Caner," short for Hurricane. The name stuck, and to this day he is still referred to as Hurricane—or Caner or Cane. So if I ever reference that name in talking about my dad, now you know why.

I don't know what happened to that hat after the game. I am sure it was eventually stomped on, but it seems like it should have been placed in the ole family trophy case with the inscription "A legacy initiated from stirring up trouble . . . The Caner Story." Or something like that. It's an origin story that should be remembered, as silly as it is. Not only does it mark my family's inaugural trip to South Bend, but it happened at a time when legends on the field were born. It was a great time to be an Irish fan, and a Canes fan for that matter. Both schools were incredible, and the matchups were electrifying. The ripple from these giants clashing can still be felt today by those who remember the glory years.

✻✻✻

In 2017, number 3 Notre Dame and number 7 Miami played as ranked teams for the first time in decades. The game carried significance because it reminded us of the once-heated rivalry between the two schools that surged in the late '80s. In fact, between 1987 and 1990, Notre Dame and Miami faced off as top-ten teams every year. In all of those games, the victor went on to win the National Championship. The matchup of Notre Dame and Miami during that run was something special. Notre Dame lineman from that era Chris Zorich told an interviewer:

That game was absolutely different. We had been looked upon as these choir boys, and Miami walked in as these renegade rebel guys, so we had something to prove. They have this legacy of having these bad-ass players kicking butt in college and then the NFL. . . . It wasn't like we were some high school team. We felt we could go toe-to-toe with these guys, where in the past, guys were scared of Miami.[1]

Now let's flash back to 1971 when the annual series started. Notre Dame dominated through the '70s. They won every game that decade. Then in 1981 the Miami program took a turn for the better by hiring coach Howard Schnellenberger. Through the '80s, the Hurricanes won six times against the Irish. The first win in South Bend came in 1984 when the two schools faced off in the second-night game played in Notre Dame Stadium. That just happened to be the very same game my father and his crew attended that kicked off the long-running South Bend tradition. It was a fateful night indeed. The Irish lost on the field, and my father lost in the parking lot. It was the beginning of a legacy for my family but the end for Coach Schnellenberger. The following year, Jimmy Johnson took over as head ball coach, and the Canes really went on a roll. "The U" as we would all come to know was born. Then again in 1985 the Irish took a beating at the hands of the Hurricanes. Coach Johnson said in an interview:

We won 58–7, and they accused us of running up the score, but we didn't run up the score. They did. They played so poorly, and we emptied the bench. We played every substitute we had throughout the whole second half of the ball game, and they criticized us for blocking a punt. They only had ten players on the field when we blocked the punt. It wasn't our doing that ran up the score. It was their poor play that ran up the score.[2]

That was the most points the Canes had scored in a game since 1967. They scored on their first four possessions of the first half and their first four possessions of the second half. The offense was unstoppable, led by quarterback Vinny Testaverde. The 58–7 loss was the worst for the Irish since 1944 when they lost to the US Army 59–0. That beatdown delivered by the Army Black Knights was an embarrassing loss that shocked the Irish nation. The head coach at the time, Ara Parseghian, said after the game, "From these ashes, Notre Dame will rise again."

That catchphrase turned into a mantra around campus that launched a historic run of success for the Irish. The next three decades that followed proved to be very fruitful for the win column. But no other team quite challenged the Irish like the Hurricanes did. The 1985 loss was still very fresh in the minds of all Irish fans as the two teams faced off again in 1987. Notre Dame was ranked number 2 and Miami was number 10. With all the build-up from the humiliating loss two years earlier, the Irish took the field with tension and hostility. But it wasn't enough. The Hurricanes were just too good, and the Irish lost again, 24–0. That defeat became another log that stoked the preverbal fire—a fire that spread from the field into the fan base, which caused some Notre Dame faithful to let frustration get the best of them.

The following year before the game, one fan took it upon himself to develop what would become the famous "Catholics vs. Convicts" T-shirt intended to harshly stereotype the Hurricanes. The media played up the Irish as good ole reverent, blue-collar gentlemen, and the Canes were portrayed as thuggish criminals—a message they ran with to hype the game and bring an exciting narrative to the matchup. On the field though that couldn't have been further from the truth. The teams had mutual respect for each other. Chris Zorich said in another interview:

> They talked about the Catholics vs. the Convicts. The players had nothing to do with that. It was just some guy who created the T-shirt. We had great respect for them. . . . The media jumped on the whole bad guys vs. good guys. For us, it was like those are our friends on the opposite side of the ball. They're good and we have to prove ourselves because before '88, we weren't that good.[3]

The players and coaching staff on that 1988 squad needed vindication from the humiliating 1987 loss, and to right the wrongs created by the whole "Catholics vs. Convicts" faux pas. There was a lot on the line that year for both the team and the university as a whole. The 1988 game would go down as one of the most controversial, albeit exciting, games in the series' history. Number 4 Notre Dame upset number 1 Miami 31–30. In dramatic fashion, the Canes scored a touchdown late in the game to put them in striking distance of a win. The confident Canes went for a two-point conversion to win the game, but Pat Terrell batted away the pass with 45 seconds to play. But that is not the play everyone remembers. The big controversy happened earlier in the fourth quarter. Miami running back Cleveland Gary fumbled on the goal line to end a pivotal Hurricane drive. Coach Jimmy Johnson said later,

> "Had we had instant replay in those days, we would have beat them four straight and won another national championship, but unfortunately it didn't work out that way."[4]

"It didn't work out that way" is right. The Irish team came to play that day, and the fans came with intense Irish spirit. They all had a score to settle with the Canes. Games aren't won or lost by a single play. In a game like that, it takes a team effort on every play to win. It takes everyone playing their best and giving it their all for all four quarters. It takes motivation and pride. It takes a heroic effort to go down in history as one of the best Notre Dame teams of all time. That 1988 squad was fiercely motivated and will always be remembered. Coach Holtz said in the locker room before the game to his players, "You've got an afternoon to play and a lifetime to remember."

That couldn't have been more true. Notre Dame would go on to win the National Championship that year, capping a classic Irish season. Fans and players alike remember that game and that season. We look back with fond memories and pride on a championship season that had a brutal schedule. The only way to a championship during those days was through Miami. They were one of the best, and Notre Dame had to face them almost every year during that era. Each game between the two schools was a classic in one way or another.

But as we all know, nothing can last forever. Administrators put an end to the series after the 1990 game when Notre Dame won 29–20. That game marked the end of a run of games between two incredible football teams. I am a Notre Damer through and through, but I have much respect for the Hurricanes. You cannot deny the fact that they were good—really good. And playing games against teams of that caliber year after year created lifelong memories that represent what is so special about the sport.

I find it germane that the very first trip my father took to South Bend, the one that started it all, was for the 1984 Miami game. He took home with him more than just a keyed-up vehicle that year. He took a new appreciation for the school, the sport, and new friends that he would have for the rest of his life. The intensity of that first game had such an impact on my father that he had no choice but to return every year thereafter to see more. Had that first game been against a mediocre competitor, it might not have had the same effect on him, and I may not be sitting here writing these stories. That 1984 game was the birth of "the Hurricane" and his legacy.

Chapter 6
Gilded Bonds

A blue 1989 Dodge Grand Caravan chugged down State Route 80 at a consistent ten miles per hour over the speed limit. Cruise control was a state-of-the-art feature in this new family vehicle. Water splashed high in response to the all-purpose tires rolling across the rain-soaked road. I was sitting in the third-row seat staring out the window. Water droplets streaked across the glass, forming a labyrinth of tiny flowing rivers that spidered out, impeding my view. My older brother, Rob, was next to me, and my cousins were in front while my father drove. It felt like we had been on the road for days. My escalating impatience led me to yell out loudly, "Are we there yet?" But no one heard me over the sports talk radio that was blaring in the van.

"Guys, how much longer?" I yelled out again.

My brother finally acknowledged me and pointed out the window. "Keep your eyes right on that tree line," he said.

I looked over and saw nothing but trees over a dark gray sky. *What is he talking about?* I thought to myself. Since he had been down this road many times before, I had to believe he knew something I didn't. This was my first trip to South Bend for the spring game, so I had no idea what to expect.

"I don't see anything," I said in frustration.

My brother rolled his eyes and said, "Just keeping looking."

Always doing what my older brother said, I kept my eyes locked on the tree line. I suspected this could be just a ploy to keep me entertained, but just maybe I was in store for something awesome. I had no idea. Suffering from a severe case of FOMO (fear of missing out), I had no choice but to submit to faith in my brother's honesty. If something amazing was about to happen, I certainly didn't want to let such a spectacle pass by.

All of the sudden, out of nowhere, I saw a bright golden shimmer peeking through the top of the tree line. Like the early morning sun breaking through stormy clouds at daybreak, a magnificently radiant structure appeared.

"There it is,", my brother said with a smile. "The golden dome of Notre Dame."

It was an amazing sight to my easily impressed eyes. I remember looking on with wonderment and awe. The infamous Golden Dome. Finally I could see it with my own eyes. A glaring beacon proclaiming we had made it to South Bend. Notre Dame was just over those trees. We were almost there. Seeing the Dome from I-80 became such a vital part of the traveling experience for everyone. The significance of that moment when the Dome presented itself was far-reaching. For me, it was a symbol of "making it"—achieving or reaching a goal. Deep thoughts for an eight-year-old, but true. That meaning has stuck with me my entire life.

I have been back many times since that first trip, but the feeling is always the same when the Dome first comes into view. A feeling of excitement, enthusiasm, and, as I got older, gratitude. Gratitude for an institution that serves as the catalyst for bringing my family closer together. In a way, the Dome became a symbol of togetherness, time spent between fathers and sons, laughs shared between friends, and happy memories made. Simply put, the Dome became a symbol of hanging out with Dad—a luxury not all people can experience. I feel blessed having that opportunity. I got a chance to know my father better, to see him away from the rigors of everyday life, to see him in a place he enjoyed. His passion for the game became my passion. It was something we could share, along with other friends and family members who had been gripped by that same genuine fervor.

As I look back, it is interesting to think about how the conversations in the car evolved over the years. As children we talked about the food in the stadium, running around the campus, and playing football in the parking lot. As teenagers the conversations turned toward the details of the game and the players. As young adults we talked coaching staff changes, projections, and scouting reports. Then as adults, after all Irish topics concluded, the conversation always turns to politics. Oh, so so so much political jarring. Driving in a car with my father, Howard, and Big Al is not without its challenges. I say that with a smile. Three old stubborn men, set in their ways, talking about the world. It becomes comical. Sometimes I just sit back with my brother and Bobby (Big Al's son) and just listen. We look at each other and laugh because we know there is nothing we can do to change their minds on geopolitical topics, even if we had strong counterpoint arguments. They are who they are, and we go for the ride.

My brother and I are basically on the same side of the proverbial coin when it comes to politics and social issues. However, my father, Howard, and Big Al are not there with us. Not even close. I am not even sure they are on the other side of that coin. They are on some ancient gold doubloon. A currency forged during a time of archaic laws and culture. There's a true generational gap in the vehicle when we're all together. Sometimes I like to kick the hornets' nest just to see what they will say. I'll bring up an election and off we go. Truthfully, I don't think it even matters what election. They have strong opinions on everything. Just pick one, show support for one side or the other—doesn't really matter which—and let them take it from there. It is more fun if you don't agree with them. That is when they get all fired up. Then they start supporting each other's arguments, and it builds and builds until there is no counterpoint left. No matter how nonsensical their political positions become, it's a guarantee that any opposing perspective will be smothered by loud jawing and short fuses. If you know its coming, which my brother, Bobby and I do, then it is fun to

41

watch. The pot starts to steam, then simmer, then boil, and right before the lid comes off, we see the Dome and are brought back to a happy place. The Dome has that effect. It reminds everyone why we are there in the first place. It evokes a social metamorphosis in which personal opinions are conceded and harmony is reestablished from the mutual sentimentalism.

Every time I see the Dome I am reminded of my inaugural voyage as a child. That first trip was very special for me. I got to see firsthand what my father and older brother had been talking about all those years. The sights and sounds of game day were everything I hoped they would be. Since it was only the spring game and not a regular season game, the stadium was not full to capacity. That meant we could basically sit where we wanted. So of course we got the best seats in the house, right on the fifty-yard line about twenty rows up. We had a perfect view of the game, easily seeing both sides of the field. More importantly, we had a great seat for seeing the tunnel on the north side of the stadium, where the players enter the field from the locker room.

It was a sunny day and I sat in anticipation, waiting for the team to run out onto the field. The game announcer came on over the loudspeaker introducing the team. They all huddled inside the tunnel for a moment before they ran out together. Like sparkling ripples on water, the gold on their helmets shimmered as they stepped into the light of the sun. The shimmering reminded me of the golden dome I witnessed poking through the trees the day before. Then it dawned on me. In that moment I realized the helmets were actually a reflection of the Dome itself. *Duh.* Prior to that I had just thought they had gold helmets because gold looked cool. Please forgive my youthful naivety. It was all coming together for me. The famous Golden Dome on campus was represented by each player's helmet. This is the first time I am admitting that was the moment I made the connection. I am embarrassed to say I didn't realize it sooner. But hey, I was just a kid. My exposure to the world was minimal.

After the game we all took a walk around campus. My father gave me the tour. When he asked what I wanted to see, my first response was, of course, the Dome. The sun was lower in the sky by the time we made our way over to it. I remember standing in the shadow of the impressive structure, peering up. The experience was dramatized by my exuberant, childlike wonderment. It was kind of like meeting a celebrity in person. Being there in that moment with my father and brother made the trip complete. For the first time I officially felt like part of the group. Something I had been hoping for back then. The Dome sealed the deal.

Today the Golden Dome is arguably the nation's leading collegiate landmark. Also known as "The Main Building," it serves primarily as a headquarters for administration, with a few classrooms still in use. This structure is actually the third building to stand on the site. It was built in 1879, the same year in which the previous building was destroyed by fire. The actual Golden Dome was added to this replacement building in 1882 and was most recently regilded in 2005. The regilding process covered the entire structure in gold leaf. The Dome is capped with a 19-foot-tall, 4,000-pound statue of Mary, the Mother of God—"Notre Dame." The Main Building is 187 feet tall, making it the second-tallest structure on campus after the Basilica of the Sacred Heart.

I learned that the tradition of painting gold on the football helmets to reflect the Dome started way back in the 1950s. Volunteers would paint the helmets before each game. The paint would actually have 23.9 karat gold flakes mixed in. The gold flakes were collected and stored for this purpose every time the Dome had to be regilded—which, by the way, happened about ten times in the history of the structure. Nothing lasts forever though. As cool as it was to have the helmets painted with actual gold, that tradition stopped after 2011. New advancements in sporting technology allowed for safer helmets that could keep their color without routinely going through the painting process. So the tradition ended, but the symbolism is still there. Every time those players run out onto the field with glaring gold helmets we are reminded of the Dome and the prestige of the institution.

To the Irish haters out there, it is just a marketing ploy. Maybe so, but you can't deny it evokes a feeling or emotion. For me it is nostalgia. The site of that sparkling cupola takes me back to a comforting place of childlike enthusiasm and jubilance. A place where all worries and stresses vanish, and I am left with a sense of connection and belonging. Whatever challenges life presents to me, I can always go back to that carefree place and calm my soul. It's the perfect fuel for balance. In the end, the Dome is just a structure, but its symbolism is a powerful tool that helps me stay focused on what is important in life. It reminds me of the importance of family and creating genuine bonds with others. Without those bonds, what a lonely world it would be.

Chapter 7
The Real Deal

There is a first time for everything. Some firsts are more exciting than others. First touchdown, first interception, first tackle, and even first true Notre Dame football game. My first game, other than those Blue and Gold games of course, was the Notre Dame vs. Stanford game. It was the perfect first game because, ironically enough, Notre Dame won its first National Championship against Stanford way back on January 1, 1925. At the end of the 1924 season, Notre Dame's Four Horsemen and legendary head coach Knute Rockne faced Stanford's Ernie Nevers and head coach Pop Warner at the Rose Bowl. This was the first time the Irish had been in the post-season. Notre Dame won that day 27–10 and proudly brought home the most coveted collegiate trophy.

My first Notre Dame game didn't have such a miraculous ending. It was October 3, 1992, and Stanford was ranked number 18 in the country. It was the first time both teams were ranked coming into the game. Stanford proved to be too much, and the Irish lost 33–16. Needless to say, I was quite disappointed. I remember walking out of the stadium after the game with my head down in disbelief, everyone around me sulking in misery and complaining under their breath. I was walking next to my father in silence. I will never forget what happened next. As we were passing through the main gates leading out of the stadium, a man passed us spewing alcohol-fueled profanity. My emotions got the best of me, and I couldn't help but repeat some of the words I heard. Without thinking or hesitation, I yelled out, "Shit, this sucks!"

The moment the words came out of my mouth, I was filled with fear. I was walking right next to my father. *Surely he must have heard me,* I thought. Not only did the Irish lose, but there I was cursing in front of my already agitated father. What was he going to do? I had never cursed like that in front of my dad before; I had no idea what to expect. He has been known to have quite the temper. Would he yell at me, smack me upside the head, or worse, not bring me back to a game ever again? In that split second so much terror and angst ran through me. My father stopped and grabbed my arm. *Oh, here we go. This is how I go out, at gate B right after a Stanford loss. Just get it over with,* I thought to myself. I accepted my punishment, and I deserved what is coming.

But nothing did. My father just stood and looked at me for a moment without a word. I couldn't tell if the anger on his face was directed toward me or the team. In any case, it wasn't pleasant. But still he said nothing, did nothing. Just looked at me. That did not stop the fear from building within my soul as my hands began to shake and sweat built on my brow. It's funny how mere seconds can feel like hours in situations like that. I made a mountain out of a mole hill as they say, because soon after I came to realize that he was not mad at my slip of the tongue. It took me a moment to understand that his silence actually communicated a different message all together. With his stern gaze he was saying, "If ever there was a time and place to curse, this was it—but never let it happen again and don't tell your mother." After that inaudible exchange, he turned and walked toward the car. Man, did I dodge a bullet there.

It was a day of firsts. My first game, the first time I cursed in front of my father, and the first time I think my father was proud of me for getting mad. Sports can do that I guess. They can bring people together both in joy and anger. People celebrate a win together and sulk in a loss together. Any other time the kind of language I heard coming out of the stadium that day wouldn't have been tolerated. But in this instance, like my father, many people would let it slide.

You know that old saying "There is a time and place for everything, and it is called college"? I think, in a way, it applies here. Now I am sure that wasn't what the founders of the university had in mind. Their intentions were almost certainly more sophisticated and honorable, and they probably wouldn't have let the outcome of a sport influence their demeanor. They had bigger plans and a higher purpose. Being the "first" for them was challenging and took focused determination. I guess that is why the university is even standing where it is today. At one point in the school's history, someone had to be the first. The first to see the potential this area had for an educational institution, the first to establish the foundation, the first to sacrifice for growth and development. There are so many origin stories that get lost, we are lucky the Irish tale of dawn still lives on.

The story goes that over 175 years ago, Father Edward F. Sorin, a young Holy Cross priest, left his native France to explore America. It was winter when he first arrived in the snow-covered Indiana wilderness. Back then it was mostly uninhabited, raw, and wild. Father Sorin was inspired and driven to establish a great educational institution dedicated to Our Lady. (Hence the name "Notre Dame.") Not long after his arrival, Father Sorin wrote a letter back to his home in France to the Blessed Basil Moreau:

> Yes, we are happy. We have the Lord with us. Only tonight we hung our sanctuary lamp where none had hung before. . . . They tell us we won't be able to afford to keep it burning. But we have a little olive oil and it will burn while it lasts. . . . We can see it through the woods, and it lights the humble home where Our Master dwells. We tell each other that we are not alone, that Jesus Christ lives among us. It gives us courage.[1]

Walking out of the stadium with thousands of people, it is hard to believe the humble beginnings of this institution. To imagine it started as a single hanging lantern with a diminishing supply of olive oil deep in the woods can help put things in perspective. As they say, a journey of many miles begins with one step. For the university, it started with that lantern. For my Irish game resume, it started with Stanford.

Chapter 8
Steel Mills and Ice Cream

A golden sun was falling behind technicolored clouds saturated with late-season oranges, pinks, and purples as it broke the horizon. I was playing a game of tackle football out in the front yard with the neighborhood kids. You know, just getting in a little extra practice before the upcoming football season. As the sun started to set behind the trees, I caught a glimpse of fireflies showing off their yellow glow, a sure sign of the dog days of summer in Ohio. My mother let us know it was dinnertime with a high-pitched whistle. The sound was so piercing that it stirred up all the dogs in the neighborhood. I really don't know how she made that super sharp sonic signal. I guess it's one of those skills only mothers have. It got our attention for sure.

My friends ran home, and I went into the house, mindful to take off my muddy shoes by the front door. I dared not track dirt through the living room or there would be hell to pay. When I walked in, my mom gave a daunting look at my grass-stained jeans before she told me to wash my hands and sit down at the table. It was Tuesday night, and the usual tuna noodle casserole was on the menu.

"It's quiet tonight. Where is Dad?" I asked, staring at his empty seat at the head of the kitchen table.

"Well, he was put back on second shift," my mother replied. "He will be late tonight."

Upset by this news, I blurted out, "I hate second shift!"

My mother was quick to respond with "Watch your mouth young man; it's only for a short while."

But I knew what "short while" meant. It meant she didn't know how long he would be scheduled this way for work. It could have been days, months, or even years. My father worked in the steel mills. It was long hours of back-breaking work. I hated second shift because that meant I would never see him. He would be at work when I came home from school, and I would be in bed sleeping when his shift ended. I was never mad at him for working that shift because I knew he had no control over it, but I was disappointed to hear the news. That shift meant we only had the weekends to hang out, which were usually so busy with the other activities my siblings and I were into. Between football practice, basketball games, band rehearsals, or karate classes here and there, we were always on the go. With dad back on second shift, he would miss a lot of those practices and games. Not only that, but his time in the furnaces always yielded a dog-tired shadow of his true self by the time the weekends rolled around.

A job like that took a lot out of a person—a reality that most people can't relate to. You can never understand what truly goes on in a steel mill until you walk through one. Deafening noise, scorching heat, razor-sharp metal shards burned off into chemical-infused air. Everything in a mill wants to hurt you. Truly hell on earth in my mind. Whenever we would discuss that "H" word in my Catholic school, it always sounded a lot like a steel mill. Every once in a while my dad would come home with a story about how someone was injured at work. That was just how things were. You never knew what would happen.

Growing up in that kind of environment really makes you appreciate the time you have with loved ones. Time is fleeting and you never know what could happen. I feel extremely blessed that my father did come home every day. Not always uninjured, but he came home. When you look at the relationships in your life that way, it makes the time you spend with others more special. That is why I loved our Notre Dame trips. Don't get me wrong—I love the Irish and I love the sights and sounds of a collegiate football game, but all that comes second to time spent with Dad. That was what our trips were really about. We never actually came out and said that, but we all knew.

Some of my favorite memories from our trips had nothing to do with football at all. It was all about spending time with family. We made it a point every night after dinner when we were in South Bend to go out for ice cream. Ice cream parlors came and went over the years, but we would always find one. Bonnie Doone's ice cream was a crowd favorite for a while, then it was Steak 'n Shake and then Kilwin's. The place didn't matter—it was the fact that we went.

I think one thing that made me have such fond memories of nightly ice cream outings, aside from the heavenly nature of frozen sugar, was seeing my father really relax and enjoy his time. At home he was always so tense and worn down from the mill. To see him in an ice cream parlor laughing and enjoying himself was the real treat. Here was this gruff man who spent his days with molten iron and steel, trying not to get scorched, dismembered, or maimed, now sitting in an ice cream parlor having a hot fudge sundae without a care in the world. It was quite an astonishing sight, and it was part of the tradition.

Even the kind of ice cream was a tradition for my father. Always, always, always a hot fudge sundae. He'd never deviate and try anything new. Maybe he just loved how sundaes mixed with coffee and cigarettes, or maybe he was superstitious that a hot fudge sundae would help bring the Irish a victory. Whatever the reason, there were no surprises. There was something very comforting about that consistency to me as a child. They always say children need routine. And as a child going to these Notre Dame games every year, there was definitely exposure to lots of routine.

That sense of consistency didn't escape us when we were home though either. My mother was a pillar of rhythmic accountability. She was up early every day, getting all us kids ready for school and out the door while my father was either recovering from the previous day's work or out early on first shift. My mother was always there running the house. She was so good at it too. As a parent myself, I can look back with better appreciation of her efforts. She was efficient, smart, and caring. Everything got done, and whatever challenges life presented to us, my mother found her way through them with flying colors. Above all that though, her patience and kindness and goodwill toward others is what really sticks out in my mind. I truly have great parents who set such a good example for us kids. They are a perfect pair—a real yin and yang. My mother with her sweet demeanor and compassion paired well with my father's grittiness and resolve. As children we inherited both of their personality traits, something we became very proud of. In life there are times that call for a softer presence and times that call for a little more muscle. We learned to embrace both.

I'd like to use this opportunity to focus on the true grit side of the coin as it relates to growth and development. I remember when I got my first job at the age of thirteen loading cement landscaping bricks into delivery trucks. Each brick had to be stacked by hand. It was brutal but I loved it. I wanted to impress my dad. I knew he valued honest hard work, and stacking bricks sure was that. I think the time I spent in that brickyard helped me discover my grittier side. I sure know it helped me on the football field. Practices were hard. We would go long hours and get yelled at constantly. But you know what? They were a piece of cake compared to the brickyard. I always compare things to those manual labor days. Nothing really stacks up from a difficulty standpoint (no pun intended . . . well maybe a little). I can only imagine that is how my father views the world as a result of spending his prime in steel mills. I can't imagine anything else really phases him now. That grit will be forever plastered to his being. A steel worker is the mascot of his life, and rightfully so.

Just like the "Fighting Irish" is the perfect representation of the University of Notre Dame. But do you know why? It has been around forever and we all just accept it. Most people don't know where the name comes from, but there are some theories. One story stands out above the rest and seems to have the most legitimacy. It goes back to the turn of the century, before Notre Dame was, well,

Notre Dame. William Howard Taft was president, the Pirates beat the Tigers to win the World Series, the Indianapolis 500 racetrack had just opened, and Notre Dame was losing to Michigan at halftime. The year was 1909, and Notre Dame was still referred to as "the Catholics." Before the team went back onto to the field to play the second half, one spritely player tried to rally the troops with some colorful words. He directed his battle cries to five players in particular. Their names were Dolan, Kelly, Glynn, Duffy, and Ryan. The agitated instigator screamed at the five of them, "What's the matter with you guys? You're all Irish and you're not fighting worth a lick." This was the motivation the men needed to go out in the second half and win the game. Upon hearing the details of the halftime pep talk, a local reporter penned, "It was a victory for the fighting Irish." Other members of the press quickly ran with the name and used it to describe the team's never-say-die fighting spirit. In all actuality, at the time, it was most likely a dig on the team intended as a derogatory term to taunt the players of the small, private, Catholic institution. A few years later a *New York Daily News* columnist put a positive spin on the term. His name was Francis Wallace, and he just happened to be a Notre Dame alumni.

The Notre Dame *Scholastic* printed an article that referenced the name as well. It read:

> The unkind appellation became symbolic of the struggle for supremacy of the field. . . . The team, while given in irony, has become our heritage. . . . So truly does it represent us that we [are] unwilling to part with it ...[1]

At the time the official nickname for the university's athletes was "the Ramblers." Then university president Reverend Matthew Walsh, seeing and hearing the press and student body using the term "Fighting Irish" as an empowering, positive symbol of grit and determination, decided to officially adopt the new nickname in 1927. And of course that one stuck.

Having an identify is a very important thing in life. I learned that from my father. He was proud to be an honest worker. He was proud that he could support his family by getting up every day and going to a brutal job to do excruciating labor. That iron grit was in his nature. Just like Notre Dame was proud to be called "Fighting Irish." Even though it was originally meant to put them down, they embraced the nature of the term, and it became their identity.

I like to think I get my identity from my father. As a child, spending time with him was special. I never knew when he might get put back on second shift (or worse). Appreciating what you have and enjoying your current moments with loved ones is truly what makes life worth living. I hope I can instill that truth into my own children, and I hope they can look back on spending time with me like I look back on spending time with my father. With excitement, pride, and joy.

Chapter 9
The "Game"

Routine becomes a part of life when you are raised Catholic. Morning prayers, church services on Sunday, and two-hand tag football games on the playground are some of the most important. My elementary school accommodated kindergarten through eighth grade in one building. It was a small school to say the least. We had a large paved parking lot that we used as a playground for recess every day. It had a drainage ditch covered by a metal grate that ran the length of the entire lot. That grate separated the boys' play zone from the girls'. I couldn't tell you what the girls did every day on their side of the playground because I was so focused on what we did on our side. No matter what day of the week or how hot or cold the weather was, the boys always, always, always played football. For those fifteen minutes a day of scholastic freedom, we ran up and down the parking lot with all the energy and intensity of a stampeding herd of buffalo. Everyone played, whether you liked the game or not. We split up into evenly matched teams and engaged in the "winner takes all afternoon bragging rights" ritualistic clash of recess warriors.

In first and second grade the games were pretty mellow, but right around third grade things started to get more intense. The desire to win increased exponentially and trash talk started. I can't tell you exactly why—it just kind of happened that way. Maybe all the boys started to feel they needed to prove themselves, or maybe some were trying to impress the girls. Or maybe football was just that big in our town. It's hard to say. I was oblivious to most things back then. I can tell you though that around that time, we all started to imitate our college and pro football heroes. I was, without a doubt, number 25, Raghib "Rocket" Ismail. He was my hero and, to this day, my all-time favorite Notre Dame football player. I used to pretend I was like Rocket tearing down the sidelines for a touchdown. I would imagine the roar of the crowd as I caught a slant pattern across the middle and took it to the house.

Being a Notre Dame fan was fun back then. There were so many electrifying players to look up to, but the Rocket was the best. He was the center of attention for all collegiate sports, and not just for Notre Dame. His popularity stretched across the country, from the Pac-12 west to the ACC east. He was truly "the man," and best of all, he wore the blue and gold. Unfortunately, when the Rocket moved on from Notre Dame in 1991 to the Canadian Football League, all of the attention shifted to the quarterback for the Florida State Seminoles. Charlie Ward, a future College Football Hall of Famer, was having a record-breaking season that year.

His name was plastered on everything. He was in all the newspapers and magazines, and the media analysts couldn't talk enough about him. He really was everywhere. Even some of the kids on the playground were emulating him. They would do the tomahawk chop and chant the Seminoles' war cry. Florida State fever started to take hold. As Ward's popularity grew on the playground, it really felt like it was us against them. And by "us" I mean the Notre Dame faithful. That only fueled tensions during our daily recess matchup. Sometimes it felt like we were at war with a very formidable foe. I can only imagine how the actual Notre Dame players felt hearing all the Seminole hype. It drove me nuts as a third-grader, so it must have actually driven them crazy.

That year, luck would have it that the Irish would have the chance to face-off against the Seminoles on the field—an opportunity to silence the war cries and maybe even bring some peace to the playground. Florida State entered the game as the number one team in the country, led by legendary coach Bobby Bowden. Charlie Ward (who would go on to win the Heisman Trophy that season as well) was primed for a big game. Notre Dame came in ranked number two in the country and was viewed as the underdog. The top two teams were going head-to-head in a dramatic midseason matchup that would be played in South Bend. Notre Dame was led by the equally legendary head coach Lou Holtz. It was called the "Game of the Century," a true national spectacle of collegiate glory. The media coverage leading up to the game was so intense that ESPN decided to broadcast *College Gameday* on location at Notre Dame Stadium for the first time in its history. (Today that traveling sports commentary show has become such an integral part of the Saturday college football experience. It is fun to think that it started because of Notre Dame, but I digress . . .)

The hype and build-up to the game was huge. Friends turned into foes, and it was every man for himself when it came to getting tickets to the game. As a third-grader there really wasn't much I could do to help find tickets (this was before the internet, mind you). You had to know someone with pull to get a seat—or be willing to sacrifice your life savings. We were fans but not stupid. My father kept my college savings in the bank and decided to watch the game from home.

About a week before the game, the university announced they would have a viewing party inside the basketball arena for fans who couldn't get tickets. This changed everything. Hope had returned for being on campus for the game. A friend at school told me this when we were playing on the playground. I couldn't wait to get home to ask my dad if we could go too. Surely these tickets fell within our price range. Unfortunately, my dad had to say no. He was scheduled to work that weekend, and it was too late to request the time off. I again was devastated. The following day I went to school with my head low, feeling the kind of unrealistic disappointment only a third-grader could have. That deflated sense of defeat did not last long though. When I walked through the classroom door, I was instantly met by a friend of mine. The same friend who had told me about the viewing party in the ACC the previous day. Before I could get a word out, he said, "Do you want to go to the ND game this weekend with me and my dad?"

I stood there speechless. Could this actually be happening?

"Well, do you?" he said again.

Upon collecting myself, I answered with an enthusiastic, "Heck yeah!"

My friend explained that the night before, his dad told him that they were going to South Bend for the game and that he could bring two friends. Tickets for the viewing party were even going fast so he had to act quickly and just got a bunch. My friend informed me that I would have to get permission from my parents first. With an overzealous reaction to the offer I told him permission wasn't necessary. I was going to that game no matter what. Asking my parents' permission at that point was just a formality. How could they possibly say no? When I got home that day, I stated my case for going to the game, and without any resistance, my parents agreed. In fact, my father was a bit envious, naturally.

That weekend we packed up the car and headed for Notre Dame. It was one of the most thrilling things a third-grader could do—embark on a road trip with two friends to arguably the best game of the century. It didn't matter to us if we watched the game live from the stadium or on a big screen in the basketball arena. We were going to be there, on campus, in the moment, to witness one of the most electrifying spectacles in all of sports. The number 1 Seminoles facing off against our beloved number 2 Irish. It was going to be an experience of a lifetime. Our expectations were through the roof.

On game day we entered the arena with popcorn, pretzels, soda, and enthusiasm. The game was projected onto a giant screen that hung from the rafters right above center court. The sound of the announcers blasted through the house speakers and reverberated off the walls. There wasn't an empty seat in the house. Everyone was primed and ready for an Irish victory. The atmosphere was electric. When the Irish took the field, the arena exploded with sound as fans came to their feet screaming as loud as they could. You know the old saying "Let's blow the roof off this place"? I actually thought that was going to happen.

We were all pumped up with the anticipation of a victory, and we were not disappointed. The Irish brought down the thunder on that cold mid-November day. Notre Dame outmatched, outplayed, and out-coached Florida State the first three quarters of play. With a 31–17 lead going into the fourth, the Irish were on the brink of victory. Florida State scored an early quarter field goal, and the Irish went conservative to try and run down the clock. With 1:39 left in play, Ward drove the Seminoles down the field. On a fourth-and-20 he completed a pass to Kez McCorvey for a touchdown. At that point I have to admit I started to get nervous.

On the following possession, Notre Dame went three-and-out, giving Florida State one more chance. Now everyone was nervous. The arena went silent when, in just three plays, Ward led Florida State to the Notre Dame fourteen-yard line. The Seminoles were in striking distance of a win, only three ticks remained on the clock, and Ward was back in shotgun, calling the signal for the final play. Upon getting the snap, he rolled out and fired the ball toward the end zone. Time stopped but my heart raced. The ball seemed to move in slow motion. Its final destination would be met with thunderous applause or overwhelming shame. In truly heroic fashion, Notre Dame cornerback Shawn Wooden reached up an exhausted hand and batted down the pass. The Irish won 31–24.

It was the end to one of the most perfect weekends of my life. The range of emotions I experienced throughout that whole ordeal was nothing short of spectacular. The anticipation of the game, the excitement of attendance, the fear of a loss, and the euphoria of a win all play a part in one of my most cherished childhood memories. You cannot live through an experience like that without coming away with an almost magical appreciation for a sport, for an institution, and for friends. In my mind, that weekend in South Bend will always live on as "The Game."

Chapter 10
Burnt in Time

D ark paneled mahogany walls enclosed the vibrant technicolored light coming through the stained glass windows. An antique carousel horse, weathered from a lifetime of creating happy memories, sat in the corner. Wafts of cigarette smoke rose to accentuate beams of spirited light that slashed across the room, cutting the space in two. An iron potbelly stove anchored the room, paying homage to the blue-collar iron industry that built this town. Wonderment filled my twelve-year-old soul as I sat in the center of a large corner booth. My father was to my right and my sister was to my left. The red leather bench stretched far enough to fit eight other Notre Dame followers. My family, Big Al's family, and Howard's family were all sitting around the large half-circle table as laughs and good conversation became the theme for that cool autumn evening at 120 North Street, Mishawaka, Indiana.

It was hard to find a dinner table for twelve, mostly children, at the restaurants in South Bend that time of year. That was why we went to Doc Pierce's Restaurant, in the next town over from South Bend. It was a small place in historic downtown Mishawaka, but it had classic comfort food, great atmosphere, and welcomed the Irish faithful. Our Notre Dame crew had been going there for years on Friday nights prior to game day. The waiters and waitresses knew our table and joined in the camaraderie. It was a happy place filled with Irish spirit. The food was served in cast iron skillets, a nod to the city's past. Mishawaka was established on the banks of the Saint Joseph River where early prospectors discovered large bog iron deposits. They determined it was a great place to build a blast furnace. Water power from the river rapids was strong enough to power heavy machinery, enabling the blast furnace to smelt the bog iron to make iron castings. The city grew around industry.

Part of the excitement of this proletarian dining experience was hearing the sizzle on the iron as the food was carefully placed in front of everyone at the table. The sound reminded everyone that touching the skillet would hurt—bad. Steam spewed into the air from each iron dish like a Yellowstone geyser. Intuitively everyone knew not to touch these mini blast furnaces. The waitstaff was probably so engrossed in our spirited dialogue that they had forgotten to verbally warn everyone about the hot skillets. A simple error that would change the course of our evening.

Big Al, engulfed in pleasant chatter, as usual, reached down to adjust the placement of the skillet in front of him. As if all his warning senses were temporarily out of order, he grabbed the side of the smoldering iron. What happened next will forever haunt me. To this day I will never forget the guttural sound that came out of that man. Part screech and part howl, it was a sound that would send shivers down anyone's spine. He launched right up out of his seat, and in that moment, I swear the entire restaurant went silent. As if time stopped, we hung in limbo for a moment, looking on in terror until a voice came out of nowhere to break the awkward silence. "Good heavens, are you okay?" the waitress who had just served the dish cried out as she tried to come to Big Al's aid. But it was too late. The damage was done. The friendly relationship we had built with the staff over years of patronage was instantly negated as heated words, hotter than the iron itself, were exchanged. Joy turned to sadness, and Irish tempers were unleashed as accusations were hurled. It was so bad that I thought our annual pilgrimage to Notre Dame was about to come to a premature end.

Everyone rose to their feet in reaction to the circumstance, but I stayed seated. In fact I slouched lower into the booth, carefully sinking away to avoid the agitated finger-pointing. Words spewed relentlessly into the air like water from a fire hose. I witnessed a grim reality take over as the happy moments we were just sharing fizzled away. Then something magical happened. A transformational sound that brought out the best in everyone. A sound that turned anger into happiness, sorrow to joy, fury to delight. A sound that everyone could get behind. Call it luck, call it chance, call it divine intervention, call it whatever you want, but right when all seemed lost, we heard the sounds of one of the greatest songs ever written cut loudly through the smoke-filled air. It was none other than the Notre Dame fight song: The great visceral unifier that takes control of your heart. A song that served as a reminder of why we were all there in that very place at that very time. The emotion-fueled storm ceased as the entire restaurant joined together in song. Grown men, women, and children alike collectively voiced the words . . .

> *Cheer, cheer for old Notre Dame,*
> *Wake up the echoes cheering her name,*
> *Send a volley cheer on high,*
> *Shake down the thunder from the sky.*
> *What though the odds be great or small*
> *Old Notre Dame will win over all,*
> *While her loyal sons are marching*
> *Onward to victory.*

The anger in the room dissipated into the refreshed air like the steam that came off those cooling iron skillets. Everyone was friends again as the familiar tune rang out loud and clear. It's a song that everyone knew and could not ignore. A song that was penned long ago and, through the years, had captured the souls of all Notre Dame faithful.

The "Notre Dame Victory March," as it is called, is one of the most recognizable collegiate fight songs. It was written at a time when industry served as the irrefutable identity for this great nation. In a year when the first passenger airplane was engineered to take flight and Henry Ford was dreaming up the Model T, two brothers completed a song that would stand the test of time. The year was 1908. Michael J. Shea, a 1905 Notre Dame graduate, wrote the music. And his brother, John F. Shea, who earned his degree from Notre Dame in 1906, wrote the words. The song wasn't actually written in South Bend. Its immaculate conception took place in Holyoke, Massachusetts in the winter of 1908. Michael played the song for the first time on the organ of the Second Congregational Church. The two brothers took the song to South Bend soon after to present it to Notre Dame officials. In the Sheas' minds this song represented everything that was pure and true about the institution.

On Easter Sunday, 1909, the song was performed in the rotunda of the administration building on campus. It was not an overnight success, though. It took some time for this classic to get recognized. It waited patiently as merely ink on paper for ten years until finally the university's marching band, under the direction of Professor Clarence Peterson, played it at an official athletic event. The song was performed periodically after that at other university-sanctioned events over the next few years. Finally, in 1928, the song was validated as the official fight song. Even then it wasn't widely known outside of campus. It was bolstered to true fame when the Irish took their athletics out on the road. When the Irish experienced success on the playing field, that enabled the song to be heard by people all over the country. Although it was almost twenty years old at that point, to the nation it was new, energetic, uplifting, and inspirational. It soon caught on like wildfire and, as they say, the rest is history.

Today nostalgia plays a bigger role in the popularity of the Victory March, but at a time when iron was rolling out of furnaces in Mishawaka, this song was rolling out in front of the Irish, fueling their unstoppable charge. Like a screaming steam whistle that sounds before a locomotive comes barreling down the tracks, this song was a warning to all others that the Irish were coming. It became a song that is loved by friends and feared by foes. Today the lyrics and music, which begin with the words "Cheer, cheer for Old Notre Dame," are in the public domain in the United States (but protected under copyright law everywhere else). Lawfully fortified into the hearts of Notre Dame faithful everywhere.

The experience of witnessing a heated situation turn instantly into a positive, joyous moment made me appreciate the Victory March even more. Upon reflecting on that day, I came to the realization that nothing is really as bad as it seems, and if you take a moment to see the whole picture, you will have a better perspective. Things can go from good to bad to worse—and then back to good again—in a heartbeat. It's better to stay centered and see the world for what it is. Go with the flow and focus on the positive. Nothing lasts forever, so it's better to enjoy the present moment and live for the now. From witnessing the events of that day, I learned that life will present difficult situations, and it's best to try to find common ground. Aggressively jawing at one another is counterproductive in most situations. I am sure the Shea brothers had no idea the song they wrote would have such a profound effect on the social development of a twelve-year-old boy in Mishawaka, Indiana, a hundred years later. But I like to believe they wrote that song with purpose, to bring people together, side by side, for the greater good.

Now the owners of Doc Pierce's on the other hand—they knew exactly what they were doing. They knew the power of that song and how it captures the hearts and minds of so many. That is why they played it loud and true. Whether that finger scorching incident had happened or not, the outcome would have been the same at the conclusion of the tune: Notre Dame pride and togetherness. Cheer, cheer for old Notre Dame.

Chapter 11
Winless Champions

"I follow three rules: do the right thing, do the best you can, and always show people you care."

—Lou Holtz

It was the summer before my seventh-grade year. You know, that transition time between middle school and junior high where the world is extremely awkward but still fun nonetheless? The solstice marked the longest day of the year, and we had just started the baseball season. All the teams in the summer league took the name of the company that sponsored them. My team was a recent addition to the league and was sponsored by a new sign making company in town. The sign shop made custom vinyl signage for businesses, schools, municipalities, and just about anyone else who had a message to communicate in a two-dimensional format. It was a small company with just a few employees, but it was generous enough to sponsor my little league team.

The owner of the company had a son, Kyle, about my age who was also on the team. I had never met him before that season, but we became instant friends. We shared a lot in common: We both were from the same town, we both were into sports, and we both loved Notre Dame. That summer league pulled players from schools all over, so even though he just lived a few blocks from me, we had never crossed paths. In fact, he had never met any of my other friends on the team either, but he fit in very well with all of us. He went to the public school, and I went to the Catholic school. Very rarely did the two schools interact. During the year, our sports teams would play against other Catholic schools, and theirs would play against other public schools. It was a time when there was a profound separation of church and state. So because of how inclusive that summer ball league was, we all made new friends during the inaugural season of the sign shop team. I learned a valuable lesson from that experience. I learned that no matter where someone comes from or what their background is, they should be given respect and accepted for who they are. People from different backgrounds can peacefully coexist and even become friends. That was certainly the case for our newly assembled crew comprised of ball players in town regardless of school, race, or religion.

Like any expansion team, we had our initial struggles. (Let's just say the win column wasn't as robust as the loss column.) But we always did our best, and everyone on the team that summer became best friends. Later, we all ended up going into seventh grade together. Even Kyle, who transferred over to my school when fall rolled around. So, all in all, I considered it a successful season. We worked hard, made new friends, and learned a sense of humility. Not to mention, since we were all Irish faithful, we had an entire summer of talking about the upcoming football season. Seriously, what else could a twelve-year-old ask for?

Hanging out with your best friends all summer playing baseball and talking Notre Dame football. The word *perfect* comes to mind when I think of ways to describe that summer. It even ended in the coolest way. Not only did Kyle's dad sponsor our summer baseball team, but he also gave us a season's end gift. It worked out well that his company made, well, signs. Since we were all big Notre Dame fans, we all got replica "Play Like a Champion" signs. I am sure he avoided breaking any copyright laws by not making the signs exactly like the original, but we all got the idea. For those in the know, this

sign is a big deal in Notre Dame culture. It's one of the most iconic
Irish football traditions. Coming out of the locker room onto the
field, the Irish players walk under a sign that reads, of course, "Play
Like A Champion Today." They tap the sign as they go by for good
luck. So we were all pleasantly surprised when we recieved our own
replica(ish) signs. I still have mine to this day. I proudly display it on
my truck when we tailgate at football games.

The sign is a special tradition started by legendary coach Lou
Holtz. It seems it has been a part of Notre Dame football since the
beginning of time, but really it has only been there since 1986. The
story goes that when Lou Holtz first got his coaching gig with the
Irish, he was sitting at his desk paging through an old book when he
came across a black and white photo of a sign that read "Play like a
champion." Being the master of motivation, he thought it was a
perfect tool to inspire his team. So he called the assistant coach,
George Stewart, into his office and asked him to go out and get a
sign like the one in the photo. Coach Stewart went to the local sign
shop, operated by sign maker Laurie Wenger, and ordered up the
ironic symbol. Three days later, the sign was made and brought to
Coach Holtz, who instantly loved it. Without any reservations, he
had the sign posted on the wall at the end of a narrow staircase
leading to the field. It has been immortalized into Irish tradition ever
since. To add to the motivation and spur further championship-
caliber effort, right above the sign is a list of Notre Dame's eleven
National Championships. This was intended to remind the players
of all who came before them. When asked about it, Coach Holtz
said:

> I told my players, "Every time you hit this sign, I want you
> to remember all the great people that played here before you,
> all the sacrifices that your teammates have made for you, all
> the people, your coaches, your parents, who are responsible
> for you being here."[1]

Coach Holtz has an uncanny knack for inspiring people to do
their best. He has the innate ability to see what drives people and
use that information for positive results. I have obviously never

been coached by Lou, so I can't say that for certain from a player perspective. But I have read his writings and listened to his speeches plenty of times to know that his words inspire me. He is a humble man and definitely someone to look up to. I think we can all benefit from finding people like that to learn from. Some folks were just put on this earth to make the lives of those around them better. The University of Notre Dame was lucky to have him. He brought so much positivity to the school, in addition to that legendary sign.

Notre Dame is not the only institution to adopt the "Play like a champion today" slogan to motivate its players. There is one other team that did the same: the Oklahoma Sooners. The University of Oklahoma has used a similar sign since the late 1940s. Their tradition was started by the coach at that time, Bud Wilkinson. Oklahoma players and coaches touch the "Play Like a Champion Today" sign posted above the locker room doors as they head into the tunnel that leads to the field before every home game. Also, the Sooners run under a crimson banner that reads "Play Like a Champion" as the team enters the field.

Many might disagree with me, but I think it is a good thing that multiple schools use this motivational phrase. I believe it is a great message for young people, and I feel as many people as possible should embrace it. It is applicable to many aspects of life and brings out the good in people. I look at it as an inspirational reminder to go out and live life to the fullest. To always do your best, whether on a field, in a classroom, at a job, or even as a parent. It is a great reminder to always put your best foot forward. I feel privileged to have been exposed to the message early in life because I have been able to use it in so many ways growing up. Positive life lessons are all around us—we just need to recognize them. We all have people we can look up to, people who inspire and motive us. Whether it's a legendary collegiate football coach or the sponsor of a little league baseball team, there are so many people out there doing their best for a better community. That is what I take from the sign, and I hope others can take something positive from it as well. The simple yellow with blue lettered sign stands as a beacon of Coach Lou's legendary recipe for success to always do the right thing, do the best you can, and show others you care.

Chapter 12
Bacon and Marinara

They say breakfast is the most important meal of the day. It breaks the overnight fasting period, replenishes your supply of glucose, and provides other essential nutrients to keep your energy levels up throughout the day. Not to mention that sitting down for a full breakfast provides the opportunity to drink an extra cup of coffee. So every day should start with this nourishing meal. That includes days in South Bend on game weekends. In my humble opinion, there is only one place to go for such fare: The American Pancake House at 508 North Dixie Way in South Bend.

Like almost everything we do, going to the Pancake House has become a tradition. Friday, Saturday, and even Sunday mornings during a home game weekend we are there. Ownership has changed over the years, but you can always count on enjoying a meal without breaking the bank, and the staff will always make you feel like you're at your own kitchen table eating a homemade breakfast. It's the kind of place you can get just about anything, from omelettes to skillets to crepes—as long as you don't mind waiting for a table.

There always seems to be a line out the door with benches full of hungry patrons. Even as an adult, there is still something exciting when the hostess calls out "Hamer, party of eight, Hamer!" It signals we're that much closer to griddle-cooked culinary bliss. But sometimes that can take a while. The wait isn't bad though because you are always among other Notre Dame faithful. They are anxiously waiting in the lobby or sitting on the benches right outside the solid oak front door, easily identifiable by their Irish gear. It's the perfect time to strike up a conversation with someone new. We've talked to people from all over the country it seems, and we found out they have the same story as us. They too are diehard fans and have been coming to the Pancake House for years, yada yada yada. It really makes you realize how much we all have in common, as a country that is. I think we forget that sometimes. We are all Americans. And what is more American than fueling up for a day of football with fried eggs and a side of hash browns and toast?

It is usually Big Al who breaks the ice and stirs up a conversation. Shortly after, we all join in, and before you know it, twenty minutes have passed, and we forget why we are there in the first place. That is, until the door swings open and the smells and sounds of a sizzling cooktop cause a sensory overload. Then we remember we are there to feast. Sometimes it's hard to break away from the conversation, mostly because Big Al is such a talker. He will sit outside all day chatting away if you let him. To be honest, sometimes that is what we have to do. After a while he notices we are all gone and gets the hint to come in and join us. He finds us easily because we always sit at the same table, back and to the right—partly because it is the only table that fits eight people and partly because I get the feeling they want us out of the way. In any case, it feels like our dedicated family table.

Like every meal we have together, as soon as we sit down, a familiar charade begins. The server will bring over waters, and before she can say anything else, my father will blurt out how Big Al is the worst tipper "so don't expect much from him," and that Howard can't hear well "so you'll have to speak up." Then usually Big Al proclaims how my father only drinks coffee, "so don't bother asking about anything else"—to which my father will reply with something along the lines of "the bill goes to that guy," pointing a grizzled finger in Al's direction. The act will continue with Howard asking multiple questions about the menu, requiring further information before he can choose what culinary direction he will head in. All this happens in that brief moment between the time the server puts the water on the table and actually says hello. It's like as soon as the water cups hit the table, the flood gates open with an onslaught of banter. Even the most seasoned server is taken aback for a moment, and their eyes suggest they must be pondering *How am I going to deal with this?* My brother, Bobby and I just keep a low profile and patiently wait for the old guys to get this routine out their systems. Once they've fulfilled their burning desire to make fools of themselves, we get back to normalcy.

Eating breakfast at the Pancake House not only quenches our appetite, but it also quenches the soul. It has become such an integral component of the traveling experience that it rivals the game itself. The intrinsic value of this mealtime goes beyond words because it is a true representation of all that is good about our trips. It is uninterrupted time to spend with Dad, my brother, and the rest of the crew. It is early in the day, a time when everyone is rested and blood sugar levels are within a normal range, leaving everyone happy and in a good mood. The prospect of a good day hasn't been tainted yet by a subpar performance on the field. It is also the only place for a meal within 200 miles that everyone can unequivocally agree on.

Choosing where to eat can be a real challenge with this group. There are many phrases that induce bewilderment around mealtime. Things like "I don't care where we go, but not there . . ." or "I'm hungry for anything, so you guys decide—as long as it has spaghetti and meatballs, but I'm hungry for anything . . ." I can go on and on with examples of these befuddling statements. They are abundant in every food-related conversation—except when we talk about the Pancake House. Like Switzerland, the Pancake House is friends with everyone. It's that cute little puppy that brings joy to your soul no matter what else is going on. It is a place we all can go back to for comfort and contentment.

I know I am making this place out to sound like God himself is the short-order cook and angels are the servers. (Which could be possible, I guess, but that is not my intention with the characterization of this place.) My purpose is to illustrate a simple fact that I have come to realize. Life can be very complicated, confusing, and sometimes impossible to figure out. Sometimes we all tend to overthink, over-rationalize, and convolute our own realities. Why do we do this to ourselves? Why do we go to that place of confusion? Sometimes the best answer is the simplest one. Sometimes all we need is scrambled eggs and bacon served up with a cup of freshly brewed hot coffee. While I try to figure out why I love the Pancake House so much, I come to a simple conclusion: It's not about the food or the atmosphere. It's about the choice. A choice that is made easily and almost instinctively. It's a path to satisfaction without barriers or road blocks. No one ever complains about the Pancake House, no one ever says "I don't want to go there." In effect, that makes the food taste better, the lights shine brighter, the smells more pleasant, and the sounds resonate amicably. Without the distraction and frustration of indecisiveness, we can all enjoy what we are really there for: spending quality time with family and friends. That is what life is all about. It's about creating moments of clarity, peace, and contentment. Why overcomplicate an already convoluted existence when you can just sit back and order the pancakes?

That same approach makes for a pleasant dinner as well. Remember how I mentioned that someone always says "I'm hungry for anything so you guys decide, as long as it has spaghetti and meatballs"? Well, those Italian comfort foods are found at Rocco's. Rocco's is a small joint located at 537 North St. Louis Boulevard in South Bend. It's one of those places that has that small town, locally owned, family-run kind of vibe. But if you aren't there for the early bird special, you better bring something to read, because you will be waiting for a while. I remember one time we set up camp outside the front door for over two hours until a table opened.

For the sake of being fully transparent, I have to admit something here. Most of the time I am indifferent when it comes to Italian food. I don't mean authentic Italian food like osso buco, ribolitta, or tiramisu. I am talking about Americanized white noodles with marinara sauce and every version of it. There, I said it. Sorry, Dad. (That combination is actually his favorite meal.) Throw in a giant meatball made from ground beef and some stale white Italian bread, and you have the "Hurricane Special."

So if the wait is so egregious and I don't like noodles with marinara, why even go to Rocco's at all? How does a place like that make the list of South Bend favorites? The answer comes down to the simple truth I mentioned earlier. I'd rather wait outside in the blistering cold for two hours than argue about where to go that makes everyone happy. With a large group like ours, those places are hard to come by. Everyone has their own opinions and tastes— which is great by the way. It's okay to have your own preferences. It just gets a little difficult to keep the train moving forward when everyone is pulling in different directions. But for whatever reason, when you mention Rocco's, everyone is in agreement.

Honestly, I don't go to South Bend for the cuisine anyway. I go to make memories. Since the majority of the group really enjoys Rocco's, then I am happy to eat there. I do enjoy the atmosphere, friendly staff, and how that place makes everyone feel overall. Sometimes you just have to let go and do what is the best for the group. I believe that is called "being a team player." So I, in turn, now love Rocco's because everyone else in our group does. That Italian gem makes for an easy dinner decision, enabling us to spend less time on figuring out where to go and more time on enjoying the fleeting moments we have together. After all, life is just a series of these moments strung together like lights on a Christmas tree. That tree is much more magnificent when each light shines bright. So, I guess what I am saying here is to make the most of each moment and do what you can to make those moments special. Forget about the small petty stuff and just eat the noodles and marinara. One day it just might not be there anymore, but you will have the memories. And you know what else? Just order some bacon with that marinara while you are at it.

Chapter 13
Friends in High Places

O ne morning, during my freshman year in college, I put on my green hoodie, grabbed my Nokia phone (the one with the bright blue Notre Dame plastic cover), and staggered out of my dorm room. It was 7:45 a.m. and my first class of the day, organic chemistry, started in fifteen minutes. It was probably one of hardest classes I had ever registered for. High school academics were a breeze, but higher education took a little more effort and focus. Those professors weren't messing around. They took higher learning seriously and worked us to the bone with the goal of getting the best out of us. For the most part, it worked. I do my best when under pressure. And believe me, there was plenty of pressure in O-chem. I wondered if Notre Dame students felt the same way. *I should ask someone who is actually enrolled at that school,* I thought to myself as I walked up Morton Hill at Ohio University. Although I had the green sweatshirt and ND phone, I was not Irish; I was an Ohio Bobcat.

The closest I ever got to being a student at Notre Dame was when I went to visit some friends there one year. They were both enrolled as premed students, so their free time was limited. But they did know how to have fun and invited me to come over from Ohio University to visit for a weekend. I drove the 330 miles from

Athens, Ohio, to South Bend, Indiana, on a Friday. I hit the road right after my last class. I met up with my fiends later that night at ND, and they showed me around campus and took me to some parties. It was fun to experience the university like a student. All my other trips there had just been for games. It wasn't even football season. Come to think of it, I don't remember what time of year it was. I just know it wasn't a game weekend. One thing I do remember was what happened when they took me to the first party. I walked through the door and was offered a drink. A guy with a green afro wig asked me if I wanted an amaretto sour. I stood there in silence for a minute. I didn't want to be rude, but I was thinking *What the heck is an amaretto sour?* Where I came from, we had Natty Light and whiskey.

"A what?" I replied. He looked back at me dumbfounded, clearly wondering how is was possible that I didn't know what an amaretto sour was.

"It's amaretto, simple syrup, and lemon juice," he said. I nodded as he poured a glass from the premade pitcher. That was my first amaretto sour, and I am proud to say that was my last amaretto sour. It's wasn't my style, but it did add something to the experience. I stuck with beer after that.

Contrary to what I had been led to believe all my life, I came to realize that Notre Dame students drank too. It wasn't all textbooks and Mass. What an eye-opening experience. I had a blast that night—one to remember. I won't get into the details because my mother will probably read this book, but I am glad I had the opportunity to hang out on campus as a student. We walked all over that night from house to house, dorm to dorm, just visiting and meeting all kinds of new people. I remember it was a challenge to get into the girls' dorms because the university had very strict rules about guys entering after a certain time. The girls' dorms even had "house moms" that we had to charm our way past. The same rules applied for the guys' dorms. When our group got there, we had to be creative in getting all the girls in. I guess that added to the excitement of the evening. *So this is what ND students do on their off time,* I thought. If I didn't have friends who were students I never would have seen the campus that way. It's good to have friends in high places.

The only other time that I came close to experiencing Notre Dame as a student came years later. To be honest this is somewhat of a stretch too. It was during a home game when the Oklahoma Sooners were in town. We couldn't get seats all together, so a few of the game tickets weren't in our usual section. I took one of the rogue tickets. I didn't really mind where I sat because I was just happy to be in the stadium. In fact, I didn't even bother to look where the seat was beforehand. I just followed the signs to my section, grabbed a pretzel from the concession stand, and walked through the tunnel to my seat. I was early, so the stadium wasn't packed yet, but my section was completely empty. Usually at least a few early birds made their way in by this point. Other sections had people but not mine. *What is wrong with this section?* I thought. Then it dawned on me: I was in the student section. Students are never early; they pour in right before the opening kickoff. I imagined they were all getting as much tailgating in as possible. Beer isn't served inside the stadium (wink wink).

When I realized I was in the student section, I figured it would either be the best game ever or the worst. Students don't sit . . . ever. They are rowdy, passionate fans that go crazy during the game. Usually I sit next to some "over the hill" alum who has somewhat mellowed with age. Sitting next to folks like that allows opportunities to sit every once in a while. That wasn't going to be the case for this game. I knew I needed to eat my pretzel quickly and prepare myself for four straight quarters of sensory overload.

When the game started, all my expectations were realized. The students didn't disappoint. They were as enthusiastic as I thought they would be. And yes, I didn't sit the entire game. Luckily I was in my late twenties, so I kind of fit in. I say "kind of" loosely. I wasn't a complete fish out of water. Notre Dame students have so many game time rituals that I had to pick up on quickly. Right from the start of the game it begins. They all scream "Go! Irish!" on the opening kickoff. They periodically dance a jig when the band plays "The Rakes of Mallow." The ones who like to show off do push-ups on each touchdown to match the score. At the end of the third quarter the band plays the "1812 Overture" as students wave their arms in unison. Their hands cleverly formed the letter K as a tribute to Coach Kelly. As of this writing he is the current coach, but from a distance I have witnessed the K, the W, and the L. And, of course, you cannot forget the complete silence for the public safety announcement. It comes in the fourth quarter when (now-retired) Tim McCarthy gave a statement over the loud speaker about the dangers of drinking and driving. He would follow the statement with an original tongue-in-cheek pun that would get the crowd laughing. It's one of those "dad jokes" that you are somewhat embarrassed to laugh at but do anyway because of tradition. It has a good message and gets everyone's attention, so I understand the delivery method. It's a great reminder that, at the end of the day, even though having fun and enjoying the game are important, safety and responsible fandom should take top priority.

After the game, all the students sway back and forth arm-in-arm as the band plays the alma mater. In the past I had seen these rituals from a distance but never up close. Every day is a school day, I guess. I watched what they did, asked questions every once in a while, and joined in. Coach Holtz once said, "I never learn anything talking. I only learn things when I ask questions." That was certainly true on that brisk October afternoon. I learned a lot about the student game rituals and what it means to be a responsible, engaged fan. Now if you were to ask me if I want to have those seats for every game, I would emphatically answer, "Not at all." It was a great experience, but I'll go back to my normal seat now.

Team Photos

Dad and I in the tailgate lot before a game.

Howard, Dad, and Al touring campus on a game
weekend wearing their standard uniforms.

The crew in the early 90s at a spring game.

Me, Rob, and Bobby after the inaugural 5K run in Indianapolis.

Me, Rob, and Dad in the tailgate lot after indulging in
those ridiculously colossal grilled steaks before a game.

Chapter 14
Behind Enemy Lines

V ast amounts of time can pass when you are not paying
attention. As I was finishing college, getting my first real
job, and starting a new adult life, I put Notre Dame on the
back burner. Before I even realized it, I had missed ten years of
adventures with the team. And by "the team," I mean my father and
company. I got wrapped up in the chaos of life and missed a big
chunk of the journey. I finally came to my senses when my older
brother was giving me a hard time about not going on the trips with
them anymore. I began to realize the fault in my ways and redirected
my efforts to make time for these trips. Thankfully, the crew was
eager to take me back. Like the prodigal son returning, they
welcomed me with enthusiasm and open arms. So I made plans to
pack up and once again rejoin the circus.

At this point I was a grown man with a family of my own. My
two young girls were still too little to come with me on these Notre
Dame trips, so I still went as a son and a brother, like I had so many
times before. I remember making the plans with my father. He said
he would pick me up at my house first thing Thursday morning. A
full day earlier than what I was accustomed to. When he pulled the
van into my driveway that morning, Howard and Big Al were

already onboard. Before the vehicle was even at a full stop, they both jumped out to greet me and my family. This action spoke volumes. It showed they really were excited for me to be back in the mix. Even though I missed so many years, I felt like I belonged. Howard grabbed my bags and loaded them into the van as Big Al struck up a conversation with my wife and daughters. My father joined in as well. But he stood at the edge of the driveway, finishing his cigarette, trying not to let the smoke get to his granddaughters. I said goodbye to my wife and the girls and jumped in the van. The feeling of excitement I had as a child going on trips with Dad found its way back into my heart. Between all the nostalgia and caffeine from the early morning coffee, I could barely sit still in the van as we pulled away.

It felt just like old times, but I soon came to realize two inevitable truths. The first was that my father, along with Howard and Al, had aged a bit in the past ten years. We all had I guess. The second was that things change. There were new routines and traditions that had been introduced during my absence. Some were more significant than others.

On my first trip back in the game in South Bend, I found myself sitting in a vehicle zooming down a back country road on a dark stormy night in early November. The windshield wipers frantically whizzed back and forth at full speed, tossing aside semi-frozen water bombs that were falling fiercely from the heavens. Dim street lights flew by creating abstract streaks of light in my peripheral vision. Lightning flashed and monstrous thunder cracked, causing the earth to shake as if we were under attack. The vehicle swayed back and forth from hurricane-like winds sweeping across the road. It was the kind of bone-chilling storm no rational person would be driving through. But a rational person wasn't driving. The man controlling that minivan on a mission was my father. Big Al was sitting shotgun, my older brother Rob and Howard were sitting in the middle row, and I sat in the back seat gripping my seatbelt tightly, trying to mask the terror that was taking me over. I thought about my wife and two small children at home. All of my fear came from leaving them on this earth alone in the event of my untimely death. I stared out the window with alarming thoughts going through my head. Things like, *Is this how I go out? Are my affairs in order? Did I pay that last life insurance premium?* The window to my left fogged up—undoubtedly from the nervous energy emanating from my soul. I used my hand to wipe a streak across the glass so I can see out. In that very moment I caught a quick glimpse of a street sign as we zoomed past. It read "Welcome to Michigan." Things had just gotten real. We were officially behind enemy lines.

Despite the madness outside the vehicle, my father stubbornly stayed resolute in his objectives as our company leader. We were on a very specific mission with a regimented timeline and a clear target. We were tactically advancing to a location very important to the three old guys sitting in front of me. I was experiencing a new custom these guys had deemed tradition-worthy years back. We were making the thirty-five-mile drive northwest from South Bend, Indiana to New Buffalo, Michigan. Years back, the three diehards (my father, Howard, and Big Al) decided to extend their Notre Dame football weekend by a day. Instead of starting the journey on a Friday before the game, the three amigos decided to go on a Thursday. This opened up time for them to explore the area surrounding South Bend. Honestly, I just think that after becoming empty nesters they were getting bored at home. They extended the trip to give themselves something to do.

My father likes to tell an origin story of what is now considered "the Thursday tradition." I can't explain it exactly like he can, but it goes something like this. Like Louis and Clark, they ventured farther out into unknown territory on those first Thursdays. Mostly all they found was farmland, but one fateful day, they found something that would change the dynamic of their Notre Dame football trips forever. While driving down a dark back country road, a bright light in the distance appeared to them like a heavenly beacon. They followed the bright light in the darkness, hoping it would lead them to something special. Like the three wisemen following the north star (albeit in their case I use the word *wise* loosely), they ventured on into the night. As the distance between them and this guiding light diminished, their spirits were filled with a calming sense of hope. They thought this light in the middle of nowhere had to be worth the journey. Then suddenly the road they were on came to an end at the edge of a dense forest. "This can't be the end of the line," they stewed. "There has to be another road. The light is still beyond these trees." They looked and looked for hours without an answer. But on that fateful night, God was watching over them and gave them a sign, a direction, a path.

When they told me this story, my imagination went wild. What was the sign? What happened? What did they see? Then I saw the sign too, and in that moment, my childlike wonderment screeched to a halt. The sign, the direction, the path they saw was literally a street sign . . . with an arrow pointing in the direction of a driveway leading into the woods. The sign was huge. It was right there at the tree line. What the heck were those guys looking for hours for? Anyway, the sign read "Four Winds Casino, this way" with blinking lights . . . and music playing. Now I don't know if it was divine intervention or just dumb luck, but those three guys had found a place that couldn't be more perfect for them to spend their Thursday nights.

At the time gambling wasn't legal in Indiana, but it was in Michigan. Since the Four Winds was the only game in town, it was able to grow at an exponential rate. The complex is huge. In addition to an elaborate casino floor, it has restaurants, bars, lounges, hotels, salons, jewelers, and shopping of all kinds. It even has a dog groomer and a car dealer. All on one massive campus. And it is the only thing around for miles. That was why the lights shined so bright in the night sky. It was kept up well too. Marble floors, clean bathrooms, helpful staff. You can even sit a drink down on a table without it sticking to any residual mystery adhesives that typically collect on unwashed surfaces. It had something for everyone. There was of course slot machines, which all of them loved; a great craft beer selection for Howard; inexpensive quality food options for Big Al; and most importantly, for my father, there was free coffee. He is the only man I know who can drink hot coffee from morning to night in hot or cold weather and not lose any sleep. And this isn't normal coffee either—it is loaded with cream and sugar. As a rule of thumb, when you are making a cup of coffee for this man, you are better off erring on the side of too much sugar. Put a couple spoons in and when you think you have enough in there, add one more. It's the kind of coffee that rivals southern sweet tea on the glycemic index. And to my father's delight, the coffee was all you can drink on the Four Winds casino floor. As long as you kept gambling, they kept the tap open. And these old guys loved to gamble—one quarter at a time, that is.

I am not the gambling type. I lose ten bucks and I'm done. But my father will literally play every slot machine on the floor at least twice before calling it a night. He moves rapidly from slot to slot, usually only playing once at each. If he hits, he may stay for a few more rounds. If he misses, he instantly moves on. Methodically drinking his coffee and smoking his cigarettes (which is still legal in casinos), he robotically slides down each row of those seizure-inducing machines, leaving a trail of cigarette butts and empty paper coffee cups in his wake. He only spends seconds at each machine, but as the night wears on, those seconds turn to minutes, the minutes turn to hours, and before you know it, it's basically Friday.

I usually just stay clear of his path of destruction and find my way to the sports grill. I pull a seat up to the bar, order dinner for one and a cold craft beer, and watch whatever games they have playing on the big screens that night. It might not seem like much, but to me that's a good time. So the Four Winds is a magical place with something for everyone. But nothing is without its flaws. The casino is in the great northern state of Michigan, which places it squarely in Wolverine country. When we crossed over that state line, the blue and gold changed to blue and maize. From a football fan perspective, we found ourselves in hostile territory. They don't like the Irish in those parts. We had made the mistake in the past of flying our Notre Dame banners high in the form of Irish apparel. Let's just say, whoever made that "Welcome to Michigan" sign on the border was full of crap. It should read "Welcome to Michigan—unless you are an Irish fan. If so, get the heck out." Now we are a little more cautious in our wardrobe selection on Thursday nights. After all, we are there to have fun, not start a brawl with Michigan folks. We save that testosterone-fueled angst for game day.

I will say though that if there were anyone I would feel confident going behind enemy lines with, it would be my father. He is not a huge guy, but he harbors a palpable quiet rage under the surface that you can sense, and it's wise to stay clear of it. Most rational people can sense this too and don't want to poke the proverbial bear. So with my father there, we are all good. If we have any trouble, we just point to him and say we are with that guy, and trouble walks away.

If only it were that easy on the football field. The Michigan Wolverines are a formidable foe and one of Notre Dame's biggest rivals. It is a matchup with a storied past—one that is exciting, yet also brutal and heartbreaking. Many years an entire football season is judged on the outcome of the Notre Dame vs. Michigan game. It's a game we take seriously as fans.

The rivalry is unlike any other because Notre Dame and Michigan rank in the top ten in both winning percentage and all-time college football wins. That is incredible when you think about it. It doesn't matter if a program is having an up season or a down, when you look at the entire body of work, these two teams are elite. They battle for that all-time number one spot, so each game matters when they take the field. It doesn't get much media attention anymore, but the stakes are higher every year. That is what makes the rivalry so exciting. The outcome of the game has a huge effect on the season with an even bigger impact on the teams' historical standings.

It is hard to believe that the first meeting of these two schools was over 130 years ago. The Civil War was still fresh in the minds of Americans, Grover Cleveland was president of the United States, Walt Whitman was shocking the world with free verse, and the Michigan Wolverines traveled to South Bend to challenge the Irish on the field for the first time. The game that occurred on the day before Thanksgiving in 1887 holds a special place in history because it was the first football game played on the campus of Notre Dame. The story goes that two players on the Michigan team sent a letter to Brother Paul, who ran Notre Dame's intramural athletics program at the time, telling him about a new game they had been playing in Michigan called "football." They offered to travel to South Bend and teach the Irish this new game. The Irish accepted—a simple act that would change the course of history for Notre Dame.

The Wolverines arrived early in the morning, and after taking a tour of campus, they all took to the field. Michigan had to teach Notre Dame the game before a real match could start. *The Scholastic*, Notre Dame's student newspaper, reported:

> It was not considered a match contest, as the home team had been organized only a few weeks, and the Michigan boys, the champions of the West, came more to instruct them in the points of the Rugby game than to win fresh laurels.[1]

At the start, players from both teams were divided evenly, regardless of school, and for the next thirty minutes, the teams scrimmaged in an effort to help the Notre Dame players get a better understanding of the game. After the Irish had a good grip on the game of football, both schools went back to their respective teams and the real game was played. *The Chronicle*, the University of Michigan's newspaper, wrote:

> The grounds were in very poor condition for playing, being covered with snow in a melting condition, and the players could scarcely keep their feet. Some time had been spent in preliminary practice; the game began and after rolling and tumbling in the mud for half an hour time was finally called, the score standing 8 to 0 in favor of U. of M.[2]

Even though it was the first game of football on campus, a large crowd formed to watch. By today's standards, the 400 to 500 student spectators that gathered around to witness this historic moment would be considered a sad turnout, but at the time, 400 to 500 was huge. From the very beginning, Notre Dame students loved the sport. After the game both teams shared a meal in the dining hall. *The Scholastic* reported:

> After a hearty dinner, Rev. President Walsh thanked the Ann Arbor team for their visit and assured them of the cordial reception that would always await them at Notre Dame. At 1 o'clock carriages were taken for Niles, and amidst rousing

cheers the University of Michigan football team departed, leaving behind them a most favorable impression.[3]

A most favorable impression indeed. The seed that was planted that day would grow into one of the winningest college football programs in the country. It was a fateful day filled with all that is great about the sport . . . competition, sportsmanship, camaraderie, and friendship.

✿✿✿

As I sat in the Four Winds as an enemy of the state, I had to take a moment to process that I was there because of an act of friendship that happened over 130 years ago—when victory was measured not by a score but by new relationships forged. Over the years, the stakes got higher and higher, and pressure built to claim the winning score, not intrinsic value. As that immense pressure continued to build, things got heated. A rivalry was formed. The two schools became the proverbial rocks of college football, each carving their own path of success in the college football landscape. So even though today the environment is harsh for the opposing team, each is stronger because of the other. So thank you, Michigan, for bringing football to Notre Dame and helping shape Irish success. A true lesson that greatness derives from forming new friendships and sharing ideas. Something I will always remember and use in my everyday life.

It is fitting that my first trip back to South Bend in ten years would yield treasured memories. Not only did I get back to my roots and return to a place where I felt so at home, with the people who are important to me, but I also had a chance to experience new adventures.

Chapter 15
Crayons and Sugar

C rayons and sugar packets were littered over the white paper table covering. Two kids' menus and four adult menus were stacked at the edge of the table, waiting to be picked up by an overworked server. Sunday morning conversations were easily overheard from the booths surrounding us in the small breakfast diner. I was sitting across from my father, talking about all the events that had happened the day before in college football. My wife was to my right and my youngest daughter was next to her, coloring pictures to pass the time until they could order their usual chocolate chip pancakes. To the left of my father was my mother, playing tic-tac-toe with my oldest daughter. Her attention was split between my mother and me. I could tell she wanted to be in the football conversation I was having with my father at the other end of the table. I included her with a childlike question: "Did you like the blue team or red team?"

This question was somewhat of a test. The blue team referred to Notre Dame of course. I am of the mind that people should make their own decisions, so I try not to push Notre Dame football on my children very much. But I have to admit that I felt proud when she blurted out "the blue team, the blue team, the blue team!" My father smiled, and I knew he was proud too. After all, he started all this.

The server brought over the pancakes for the kids, and their attention shifted to the melted chocolate chips cooked inside. Like digging for buried treasure, they went after the sugary morsels and were temporarily entertained. My father and I got back to talking serious football. It was the week before the Notre Dame vs. USC game, and my father was telling me he might get tickets to the game. That was exciting news. It was the big game that year. Both teams only had one loss at that point in the season, so the outcome of this particular game was very important. I was excited for him to have the opportunity to go to an event like that.

Being a busy father and husband myself, I could not go. Although I loved Notre Dame football, my family had to come first. When I mentioned out loud that I could not go because of prior family commitments, my mother's eyes rose from her tic-tac-toe game, and she joined the conversation. I knew what she was going to say. I could see it in her eyes, she was about to tell a story that I have heard a thousand times but was always entertaining from my point of view.

"See Bob," she said, "Mark has his priorities straight." My father smiled and rolled his eyes. We all knew where this story was going. My mother loves telling it, and we love hearing it because it demonstrates the dynamic between a couple who has been married for fifty years. My mother spoke and my father sat in silence, like a puppy being scolded for chewing the furniture. He knew he was in the wrong and would never hear the end of it.

The story goes that when I was about four, my mother was nine months pregnant with my younger brother David. She was due to go into labor at any time. While she was packing bags for the hospital, my father was packing bags for Notre Dame. He had tickets for the Notre Dame vs. USC game that year. In his mind, he would travel to South Bend on Friday, catch the game on Saturday, travel back on Sunday, and be there for the birth of his fifth child on Monday. Now, in my mother's mind, he would travel on Friday, and she would go into labor on Saturday. She would be forced to ask my older brother, who was twelve at the time, to get her, my two sisters, and me (with all our stuff) into the family vehicle, then figure out how to operate the Chrysler minivan well enough to drive all of us to the hospital in dramatic fashion.

My father had never missed a game, especially one of that magnitude. He was determined to go. My mother didn't care; she was determined to keep him in town. I have to side with my mother on this. My father ultimately made the right choice and stayed home. Good thing he did because my brother was born that Friday. When my mother tells the story, she starts by saying, "Bob almost missed the birth of his child." When my father tells the story, he starts by saying, "The only year I missed a game was the year David was born." Whenever we hear my parents tell the story together, it is always entertaining to see all the eye rolling that happens. I am sure that at the time there was much tension between them, but after thirty years, their attitude about it has become much more playful. Everything worked out.

As a child I always asked myself what was so important about the Notre Dame vs USC game that would make my father chance missing his own son's birth. As I grew older and became a bigger fan of the Irish—more than just rooting for "the blue team"—I learned the Notre Dame vs. USC game was a special rivalry between two schools that don't share geography or a conference. Separated by over 1,500 miles, these gridiron foes come together on the field to produce one of the biggest intersectional rivalries in all of college football. The game adds a unique narrative to American sports and has a rich history that goes all the way back to 1926. In that first meeting, Notre Dame won a thrilling game by a score of 13–12.

There are a few stories out there that chronicle that first meeting of these college football titans. The first story is called a "conversation between wives." In this tale, the wives of Notre Dame head coach Knute Rockne and USC athletic director Gywnn Wilson met in Lincoln, Nebraska, where Notre Dame was playing Nebraska on Thanksgiving Day. The Wilsons traveled to Lincoln that day to try and convince Irish decision makers to put the Trojans on their football schedule in an attempt to get USC national attention. At first Knute Rockne was not thrilled with scheduling

USC because of the travel involved, but Mrs. Wilson was able to persuade Mrs. Rockne that a trip every two years to sunny Southern California would be a nice escape from the cold, snowy Indiana winters. Mrs. Rockne was sold and convinced her husband to schedule the Trojans. That fateful meeting of wives started what we now know as one of the best rivalries in college football.

Another tale tells a different origin. It says that the Irish were gaining so much attention, coming off their 1924 National Championship, that they were having trouble getting teams to play them. Especially in the Western Conference, which is called the Big 10 today. The Irish received interest from the Rose Bowl Committee to have Notre Dame come and play a Pacific Coast Conference (now Pac-12) opponent. Coach Rockne and the Notre Dame administration realized how lucrative an annual trip to Los Angeles would be for the football program. The matchup was arranged as a home-and-home series, meaning one year the game would be played in Los Angeles and the following year in South Bend. Today the game is scheduled on the Saturday following Thanksgiving Day when it is played in Los Angeles or on the third Saturday of October when the game is played in South Bend.

It is debatable which story is true, although one is a little more romantic than the other. In any case, what came after that first meeting is truly legendary. The matchup became a rivalry because of the success both programs had over the years, with both schools having won a combined twenty-two National Championships and produced fourteen Heisman Trophies. It was that success that made the game so popular among fans. Tickets were hard to come by, and the chance to see the game in person was the chance of a lifetime. That is why my father had his moral dilemma on that third Saturday of October. Having to choose between football and family weighed heavy on him. Ultimately, he made the right choice to see the birth of my brother. (Although it would have been a great game to see, with Notre Dame winning 37–3.)

My mother did not care that the Irish, in spectacular fashion, switched to green jerseys during halftime of that game and ran out of the tunnel behind head coach Gerry Faust to thunderous applause. She was happy my dad was there to hold David, but she still to this day, for good reason, needs to give my father grief.

So there we were some thirty years later. My father had the chance to go see a classic in the making. He has been to many games in Notre Dame stadium, but none of them were when the Irish were facing off against the Trojans. I don't know if it's because he could never get tickets or he was just afraid of how my mother would react. That matchup in particular really fires up my mother. You need to be careful when you reference Notre Dame vs. USC around those two.

After years of shame my father built up the courage to say out loud something I never thought I would hear. He said, "I'm finally going to see Notre Dame versus USC." He then followed it up with an even more surprising question. "Do you think I should ask your brother, David, if he wants to go?" While this exchange was taking place, my youngest daughter picked up her crayons and started to draw a family picture on the paper tablecloth. I happened to glance over and caught a look at her masterpiece. She was very thorough in her interpretation. You know how they say art imitates life? Well her depiction of our family was spot-on. I asked her to explain the picture to me and she was happy to do so. She said, "This is Grandpa and this is Grandma. Grandma is really mad and Grandpa is scared." It's funny how kids pick up on everything, isn't it? It's even funnier when they visualize their interpretations with red and blue crayons on a restaurant tablecloth.

Chapter 16
A "Lot" of Fun

I t was 5:00 a.m. on a brisk autumn morning. What had once been dew on the ground two weeks prior was now frost. The seasons change abruptly in northern Indiana. I awoke in my hotel room to the sound of the Notre Dame fight song playing on my smartphone. The night before I had set my alarm to play that tune as a reminder that it was game day in the morning. An early wake-up call, on a Saturday no less, was necessary to get the perfect spot in the Notre Dame tailgate lot before anyone else. Not an okay spot or even a good spot. I needed to get the *perfect* spot. A spot that backed up to a grassy section so I could open the tailgate of my Chevy truck and set up chairs, tables, and a grill. A spot that was close to an exit so that when the mad rush to vacate the lot came at the end of the game, I could do so with ease. These were all very important factors. Some might say I am OCD about this, but when over 50,000 people pack into a lot, you want as much control as possible. I've picked up a few tricks over the years, and that is why I get up at 5:00 a.m. to drive my truck down to the lot to find that ideal spot that will be our home for the next sixteen hours. There are plenty of people who have the same idea as me. So I have to be quick, decisive, and relentless with my resolve.

When I roll into the lot around 5:15 a.m. I see the true professional tailgaters. The real diehards with their elaborate setups put me to shame. They are dedicated, passionate, and I respect their drive. It is not uncommon to see TV satellite dishes, tents, barbecue smokers, generators, flags, cornhole, and coolers upon coolers of food and beer—all of which are tricked out in fantastic blues, greens, and golds. It's as if a giant magical leprechaun has vomited Irish spirit all over the lot. It's truly an amazing sight—and that's before the sun has even come up yet!

Rising early and getting straight to work is a lifestyle I adopted from my father. I can recall plenty of instances growing up when it was a requirement. I was taught to get out of bed before the sun rises to get the worms for a day of fishing on the lake with Dad, to be the first one to sports practices to get in some extra work, and to show up before anyone else on the job to maximize productivity. As I look back, I realize that was my father's voice in my head telling me to always go the extra mile. So it is only fitting that I bring the same determination when it comes to getting the best spot in the tailgate lot. After all, I can't disappoint Dad.

I can sum up the experience in the Notre Dame tailgate lot before games in one word . . . FUN. It is a time to kick back and enjoy all that is great about Notre Dame football. The sounds and smells are therapeutic and help take my mind off the stresses of everyday life. The air is saturated with aromas of grilled meat and fresh beer. The sounds of sizzling steaks, laughter, and Irish cheer can be heard for miles. We are all friends here, and on game day we are all Irish.

Even as an adult I still love to throw the football around. It allows me to get some light exercise in before I consume 5,000 calories of slow-cooked bliss. My father, Big Al, and Howard always seem to find an acquaintance and invite them over to our on-demand feast of chips and burgers. The food table becomes a community table really. The same applies to the tailgaters around us. We all mingle and share food and stories. It's a real social environment. This tailgate extravaganza taught me how to raise a glass with strangers and make new friends. I am excited for my children to get a little older and come along on these adventures with us. I want them to not be afraid to meet new people and carry on meaningful conversation. Being around like-minded individuals enriches our lives. I want them to see that for themselves.

After all the pomp and circumstance, when everyone is packing up to head over to the stadium for game time, we have one last ritual. That ritual comes in the form of a gut-busting 16-ounce steak. Every year Howard stops at the local butcher to acquire the best cuts of meat money can buy. It is his special gift to all of us, and it is nothing short of amazing. We unleash those prime cuts from their white paper wrapping and toss them on the grill. Smoke rises into the air, and the smell of perfection isn't far behind. Bystanders look on with envy. The steaks are served up on plates with no other culinary distractions. Before each of us is just a plate of meat the size of our heads. We take a moment to appreciate the sacrifices made to have this wonderful indulgence. Both the sacrifice of the cow and the financial sacrifice Howard made to get us those delicious man-sized meals doesn't go unnoticed. Our knives cutting effortlessly through New York strip is the crowning moment of our ceremonial pregame routine. You definitely have to just live in the moment when it comes to these steaks. If you think about the repercussions of consuming such a monstrous amount of cow, you might not enjoy the fact that it is all yours.

So we eat without a care in the world, wash it all down with a cold beer, and just sit for a second to bask in the victory of defeating such a beast. I understand heart-healthy habits are a top priority when trying to live a long, fruitful life, but in those moments, I don't care. I'll worry about recommended caloric intakes another day. Game day is about having fun, enjoying the moment, and spending quality time with Dad. They say there are a few things you can never get back; a stone after it's thrown, a word after it's said, and time after it's gone. I want to make the most of the time I have with my family and take nothing for granted. After all, any day could be our last. So this tailgating fun is justified by the fact that we all can share these moments together and look back with fond memories.

Chapter 17
A Revealing Run

It was one of those crazy early mornings in South Bend that involved waking up at 5:00 a.m. on game day to lay claim to the best tailgate spot I could find. Big Al's son, Bobby, and I drove into the J lot and found a spot easily. The Miami (Ohio) game wasn't starting until 5:00 p.m., so the lot was empty. Since we found the spot so effortlessly and it was so quiet, we decided to go for a run around campus. Up and down back roads and through quads we ran, enjoying the peacefulness you don't normally experience on a game day. We stopped at the Grotto of Our Lady of Lourdes to say a prayer. It's a sacred place carved into the side of a hill on the northwest side of campus. Lined with hand-placed stone, the grotto is a one-seventh–sized replica of the famed original shrine in Lourdes, France. On February 11, 1858, the Virgin Mary first appeared to Saint Bernadette at that sacred location in Southern France.

Saint Bernadette was fourteen years old when she claimed to be visited by the mother of Jesus Christ. She would go on to claim eighteen more visitations that year in the same rocky, cavelike spot. She explained that the Virgin Mary had revealed herself and asked that a chapel be built on that site. The Virgin Mary told the young girl to drink from a fountain in the grotto, but no water was to be found. Saint Bernadette eventually found an underground spring when she dug into the earth below. Today millions of people flock to France to visit Saint Bernadette's grotto. Notre Dame University founder Father Edward Sorin reproduced the French site on campus in 1896, thanks to a gift from Reverend Thomas Carroll, a former theology student. The stone boulders used to construct the shrine were sourced from surrounding farms, most weighing two tons or more. A small stone from the original grotto in France is located on the right-hand side of the shrine directly below a beautifully lit statue of Mary that sits in a small carved out cavern 20 feet above the ground. Hundreds of candles line the interior walls. In the early morning hours before the sun comes up, it is an amazing sight. Each candle burns bright, and from a distance they appear to unite into one magnificent luminary in the dark night. Like an intricate crystal chandelier, it paints the surrounding area with shimmering beams of light. The shrine is surrounded by wrought iron kneelers, making it a perfect place for meditation. A wooden sign reads "Rosary prayer every day at 6:45 p.m."

After paying our respects at the grotto, we continued our run on the trail that follows the shoreline of Saint Mary's Lake. In the early days the lake provided food, ice, marl for brick, and water for steam to support university operations. Now a trail surrounds the picturesque lake that serves as a nature preserve. As we ran, fog rising from the lake slowly drifted from west to east. The natural beauty made me forget we had ran about five miles at that point. I was actually exhausted, but this unique perspective of the campus energized me to keep going.

We passed "The Rock," a building constructed in memory of Knute Rockne. Knute was Notre Dame's football coach from 1918 to 1931 and, by percentage, the winningest coach in college football. The building opened in 1937 and contains a bronze bust of the legendary coach. Fans and students started the tradition of touching Knute's nose for good luck. The bronze bust is tarnished and shows its age but the nose looks shiny and new from all the people trying to boost their fortunes.

Nowadays the university is constantly expanding and evolving with renovations and new structures. As we continued our run through this ever-changing landscape, we came across some interesting new construction near the stadium. I would later find out what we were looking at was part of the Campus Crossroads project. That project included three new buildings: nine-story Duncan Student Center (a study, fitness, career counseling, and student activities building on the west side of the stadium), nine-story Corbett Family Hall (an anthropology, psychology, and digital media building on the east side), and O'Neill Hall (a six-story music building on the south side). Construction wasn't complete yet but looked finished enough, sparking our interest to see what was inside. The sun still hadn't risen yet at this point so interior lights shining through the windows indicated which floors had power and which floors didn't. Two student guards wearing yellow security vests had a post at the front door of one of the buildings. Probably to keep out folks who shouldn't be there, but we confidently pretended we had business in the new building and walked right in. No questions asked. Honestly I don't think the student guards were on high alert at 5:30 a.m. We walked around uninterrupted, looking at all the new labs, classrooms, and lecture spaces. It appeared state-of-the-art with all the visible fiber optic runs and spaces obviously designed for collaboration. The layout of the building was somewhat maze-like, and we found ourselves getting turned around pretty easily.

We opened an unmarked door, thinking at best that it was another classroom. But not this door. This door led right into the stadium. *Could this be true?* I thought as I walked through. In the still of the early morning, no one was there to stop us. We walked right in, and what I saw completely changed my perspective of the place. Opportunities like this were rare, so we decided to see as much as we could. I am sure we were breaking all kinds of security rules, but at that point we could have cared less. We walked around the inner corridor of the stadium, into the bleachers and, yes, onto the field. The same field where so many of my childhood heroes played. Following Bobby's lead, I ran the length of the field, starting in the south end zone, across the blue and gold Notre Dame logo at mid field, then through the north end zone. Filled with so much energy,

I continued running up the bleachers and back into the concession area. I kept running just like Forrest Gump. Nobody was there to stop me.

I felt like I was seeing the stadium for the first time all over again. Memories started to flash in my mind as I took in the silence. I had never experienced the stadium like this before. Not a single person in sight. Up to that point, every time I was within those walls I was accompanied by thousands of people. Because of all my past encounters, I was conditioned to experience this place as a part of a crowd. But not this time. This time I was a crowd of one.

While taking my own personal tour, I took a long look at the seating section posters and had a chance to appreciate them as art. Each poster, designed to look like a historic ticket stub, nostalgically hung above each section entrance, capturing a snapshot in time. Section 19–22 Notre Dame vs. Wisconsin, October 6, 1928 . . . Section 13–14 Notre Dame vs. Ohio State, October 31, 1936 . . . I was surrounded by iconic stories of the past, and for the first time, I could hear the echoes. I imagined what the sights and sounds would have been—the announcer's call of the game, the roaring crowd, derby hats and hip-length cardigans, fresh popcorn and tobacco smoke. Images of the past filled my mind as if I were magically transported back to the glory years. I imagined I was attending a game with a Knute Rockne-coached Irish team. His ironic halftime speech played back in my mind, and I could hear his words: "And don't forget, men: today is the day we're gonna win."

I had a new appreciation for the stadium. To imagine what those walls had seen was a thrilling experience. It is something every Notre Dame fan should do. I hope everyone can take the time to walk around the stadium and use their imagination to be transported to a moment in history. I hope they can take in the sights and sounds and truly appreciate the Americana that is present there. It can be very therapeutic and puts things in perspective.

That idea can be applied to so many other things in life. I think we owe it to ourselves to always take a step back and look at the big picture, to put things in perspective, to stop and smell the roses as they say, and enjoy the present moment. I think too often we worry about what will be and not what is. I am certainly guilty of that too, but I am trying to appreciate the "now" a little more. Our early morning run revealed much to me that day. It not only let me see the campus and stadium like never before, but it enabled me to take a peaceful look inward and see truths that I will forever remember.

Chapter 18
A Series of Shamrocks

Have you ever been in a new place, somewhere you know you have never been before, but something was eerily familiar, as if you had walked that same path hundreds of times? That is how I felt as I was walking under a bridge in downtown Indianapolis. It was my first trip to this Midwest city. Peyton Manning was mayor, town priest, police chief, and every other position of authority at the time. The city was painted in Colts royal blue and white, and the horseshoe symbol was proudly plastered on everything. I was walking under an I-70 overpass, the interstate that circles the city. A street performer was wailing away on a saxophone. The sound reverberated off the walls like an echo chamber and filled the air with full, rich sound. It was fascinating to hear the clarity and power that came from a single instrument. The musician was very talented so I tossed a few bucks in his hat as I walked by, as did many others before—like we were paying the gatekeeper for passage to what we would see next.

It was the middle of the day, but under the bridge it was dark. Only a few yellowish-green cast street lamps sporadically lit the way. In and out of shadows I moved. The bridge was long and felt more like walking through a train tunnel, but I could see a bright light at the end. I instinctively walked toward it. As I approached the clearing, the light was so luminous I had to shade my eyes with my hand. What lay just beyond was hard to distinguish at first. As my eyes readjusted to the daylight, the music of the saxophone behind me seamlessly blended into a familiar sound in front of me. Clarity of place returned as I looked out over the Pan Am Plaza. The familiar sound I heard was the Notre Dame band; the royal blue and white had changed to navy, green, and gold. The smell of sizzling steaks on a grill filled the air, and the warmth of the sun on my face all contributed to an instant gratifying feeling of arrival. I had entered what I can only describe as a traveling circus. The only thing missing were fire breathers and seals balancing beach balls on their noses. I was in Indianapolis, Indiana, a city I had never visited before, but it felt just like being in South Bend. I had just entered Friday's main attraction for the Notre Dame Shamrock Series game.

The Shamrock Series is Notre Dame's home-away-from-home game series, a relatively new tradition started in 2009. Each year the team plays a home game in a destination city other than South Bend. They use one of their designated home scheduled slots to pack up the team and travel to play at iconic stadiums. It is still considered a home game for the Irish, albeit everyone migrates to places like San Antonio, New York, Washington DC, Chicago, Indianapolis, and Boston. The Shamrock Series is intended to give fans an entire weekend of festivities on the road while preserving the home game experience. Thousands of people attend the traveling pep rally, band concerts, Mass, Fan Fest, and even the traditional 5K run. It is also the game where the Irish break tradition and wear those one-time-use jazzed up uniforms. Each year is different with custom-designed threads that bring a new level of youthful excitement to the game. The series became an opportunity for Irish faithful to explore a new city and experience Notre Dame football home game traditions in an incredibly unique and unforgettable way. Indianapolis had become our home-away-from-home for this year's game. A new city that felt just like South Bend.

The Friday Fan Fest we had just entered was overwhelming. Much like ESPN's *College Gameday*, thousands of screaming fans wielding homemade signs surrounded a stage of sports commentators as TV cameras on jibs flew overhead to broadcast the event. Right behind that were the beer and food trucks wafting delectable aromas into the air. I had just eatten breakfast, but a steak sandwich with peppers and onions and a cold pilsner were calling my name. Continuing on behind the food section was the fan activity area. Adults and children alike were getting their pictures taken wearing a gold helmet in the photo booth. Others were running the football-themed obstacle course. There were even football team alums stationed to sign autographs. It was a bustling playground for Irish fans and it was only 9:00 a.m.

This was the first time we had all decided to break tradition and go to a Shamrock game. I was skeptical at first, but after witnessing how much the university really put into the event, I was happy to be there. I am not ashamed to admit I was one of those adults who put on the Irish football helmet and ran the obstacle course. I got completely smoked though by the ten-year-olds I was competing against. Who cares, right? It was all in good fun. After the morning steak sandwich and a few beers, my aim was a little off when I tried to throw a football at the official Miller Lite target.

As I was busy trying to relive my youth, my father, Big Al, and Howard somehow talked their way onto the broadcast stage. They were standing next to the sports commentator bench chatting it up with the analysts. I couldn't tell from where I was, but I believe there were a few old players up there too. I took off the gold helmet, leaving behind my ten-year-old self, and made my way over to the broadcast stage where Dad was. By the time I made my way through the crowd, the three of them were already off the stage. They were laughing and chatting about what had just happened. I think they were in disbelief of how they had managed to charm their way into a live broadcast. Right as I got there, a local TV crew, who was covering the event, approached the three of them for a live interview. It was like these three Irish veterans were celebrities. The world presented them with their fifteen minutes of fame then threw in a few extra just for good measure.

I am not sure why the news crew approached them. There were thousands of other people there all dressed in Notre Dame swag, grinning ear to ear. Maybe the news crew noticed the three of them on stage moments before, or maybe they could just recognize diehard fans. In any case, the reporter asked the three of them to stand together as she put a mic in their faces. They were all too eager to disclose the thoughts that were firing in their collective brains. Words spewed from their mouths like a firehose. In that short five-minute interview, they talked about their thirty-plus year history going to Notre Dame games, their hometown of Youngstown, political views, their stance on major social issues, then back to Notre Dame football. They rounded out the interview with a few bad jokes and a big thank you. I am not sure if it was the easiest or hardest interview for this reporter. I use the word "interview" lightly because there really wasn't a back-and-forth exchange. The reporter basically just asked them their names and they took it from there. Like a snowball rolling down a steep hill, gaining momentum as it goes, words from the three of them entered the air at an exponential pace. The reporter just gave them a nudge with a softball questions up front and off they went. Once the preverbal snowball was barreling down the hill, the reporter was powerless to stop it. She just had to stand there holding the mic out and nodding until the avalanche of vocabulary lost momentum and came to a natural rest. With a somewhat confused expression, the reporter said thank you and went on her way. Afterward, the three of them proudly looked at each other with chests puffed out like turkeys displaying dominance.

"I think that went well," said Big Al.

"Yeah, really well," said Howard.

My father just nodded and lit a victory cigarette—and why not? It has been a whole six minutes since his last one.

In that moment, I felt proud of the three of them and thankful to be part of this group. Here were three old best friends still doing what they loved with childlike enthusiasm. It was one of those internally moving moments for me because just ten minutes earlier I had tapped into my own childhood existence to put on that gold helmet and run the obstacle course as a grown man. While looking through that steel face mask, I wondered if I should feel embarrassed to get excited about participating in childish games, but that idea was squashed when I witnessed these three guys embracing that youthful excitement from their own experience. I guess you could use the old saying "The apple doesn't fall far from the tree," in this scenario. For me it was one of those moments where I realized I am my father's son and proud to be so. Witnessing their interview might have seemed like a simple thing, but it had a deeper meaning. In that moment, I experienced thoughts of family, tradition, youthful excitement for life and enjoying the present with no reservation—an experience I may not have gotten had we been in South Bend. Don't get me wrong, I treasure my experiences when home games are on campus, but this was different and worth the effort.

We continued to explore the Fan Fest and came across the tent that displayed the Shamrock Series uniform the players would be wearing. That year the uniforms were created by Under Armour and a lot of storytelling had been incorporated into the design. The theme of these unique uniforms was the Golden Dome. Traditionally the helmets are always gold, a tribute to the Dome, but Under Armour took that a bit further. The Golden Dome has a natural crosshatch texture where the metal plates come together to form the curves of the structure. That same pattern was represented in the helmets. It was subtle, but close-up you can see the intricacy of design. A blue stripe went down the center of the helmet and the ND logo was on both sides. The jersey was a solid dark blue with gold sleeves. A sophisticated Irish mosaic design was stitched into the fabric, a detail that mimics the mosaics inside the Dome. When you walk into the Main Building, aka, the Golden Dome building, beautiful tile mosaics are featured on the floor and ceiling. These mosaics inspired the patterns on the jerseys that year. The uniform pants were solid blue with a gold detail above the knee, and the shoes were a shimmering solid gold to round off the look. It was an impressive design, and, of coarse, we had to take our picture next to it. So my father, older brother, and I waited in line with the other children to get our chance to take a photo with the uniform. I have to admit it was a little childish, but it did make a memory. After all, that is what our trips were all about.

It is those kind of simple, authentic moments with my father that I cherish and can only hope to share similarly with my own children. I learn a lot about good parenting on these trips. I witness firsthand that the simple act of being present in the current moment as a parent is so important to making an experience memorable. Sharing that time with my father and brother helps me appreciate family and where I come from. We are all grown men with different views on life, but we stood by the Shamrock Series uniform display unified in a common interest. Something so simple but so powerful. When I look back on it, I laugh when I think of how a football uniform can inspire such an experience.

We left the Fan Fest and began to explore the city. Walking up and down streets, stopping in breweries that looked interesting, and just chatting. We had no plans, nowhere to be, just moving at our own pace and seeing what we could see. Of course, as with every trip, we had to stop in places to get souvenirs for the family back home. That was the only true "must-do" for the day, otherwise we were free to roam. In our wanderings we came across a huge open-air market full of food vendors and merchants. The sheer sprawl of this place and quantity of the merchants was overwhelming. I didn't know where to begin, so I just walked aimlessly.

While looking around the market I saw signs that read "Notre Dame 5K Registration." *Now that is interesting*, I thought. We were far from the Fan Fest, but Irish events were still being planned across town. We decided that since we were there, we might as well check that out too. When we got to the registration table, three volunteers were feverishly working. Getting people signed in, distributing maps and water bottles, giving directions to the hundreds of people that were waiting in line. *Could all these people be here just for a run?* I thought. The line was moving quickly, so on a whim we decided to sign up. My older brother, Bobby, and myself took on the challenge. The run was scheduled for the following morning, game day. We found out it was a Shamrock Series tradition, which gave us even more motivation to participate. We signed on the dotted line and committed.

We broke tradition the following morning by not waking early to get to a tailgate lot. However, we did wake up early to get ourselves to the 5K run on time. Sign in was at 8:00 a.m., and we were there right on the dot. The course went all through downtown

Indianapolis and began and ended at the Bankers Life Fieldhouse. The Fieldhouse is where the Indiana Pacers play home games, so naturally the building was covered with Pacer blue and yellow. Not quite Notre Dame colors, but close enough.

Along with about two thousand other runners, we gathered outside on the street at the start canopy. As we waited for the start gun to fire, I was able to do some interesting people watching. It was a mixed bag of individuals who collectively made the event feel more like an Irish-themed Halloween party than a run. Some were dressed as leprechauns, some were painted head to toe with green body paint, and others wore Irish leisure suits. It is quite a festive group, and I anticipated an entertaining run. It had topped out at about forty degrees, so many folks were jumping up and down or running in place to keep warm. Everyone was anxious to get started, myself included.

At the stroke of 9:00 a.m. the gun fired, and off we went. Some people sped quickly to the front of the pack and others just leisurely walked. We were somewhere in the middle. Our goal wasn't to get personal best times or anything like that—it was more about the experience. We ran up and down streets then in and out of alleyways. Even though we were downtown, the calmness of the early morning was relaxing and peaceful. Shop owners were just unlocking the doors to get commerce started, street sweepers were wrapping up their duties cleaning from the night before, coffee houses and bakeries were emitting heavenly scents into the air as they prepped for the morning rush, steam billowed from vents in the ground into the cool morning air. The only sounds that could be heard were my running shoes hitting the pavement. I got lost in the moment, focusing on my breathing and simply enjoying the "now." We had the opportunity to view this city in a very unique way— something we wouldn't have experienced had we not decided to go to a Shamrock series game and sign up for a 5K run. I know I sound like a broken record when I say this, but that is what I treasure about these trips. It's not just the game; it's the experiences and memories made.

As we got closer to the end, the Notre Dame marching band split up into groups and took post at different street corners. They played Irish music, encouraging everyone to keep at it and finish strong. It was a very empowering gesture and just what we needed to pick up the pace and finish with our best effort. I imagine, to some degree, that is what the team on the field experiences when they hear the band playing the fight song in the stands. Just a little extra motivation to keep going. As we got closer to the finish line, the street was lined with supporters clapping and cheering us on. We make a turn onto the homestretch, and there was a giant running clock displaying our time. Right under it was my father, smoking a cigarette, of course. He stuck out like a sore thumb as the only smoker in the crowd at this health and wellness event. But he was there. He had woken up early enough to see his sons finish the race. It was definitely not his scene, but he came anyway to support us—something good fathers do. I was happy to see him standing there, encouraging us in his own way. Smoke swirled around him from the gusts produced by other passing runners. As I ran past him he reached out a hand for a high five, symbolizing approval and accomplishment—the very things that every son desires from their father.

We finished the race at the same location where the Fan Fest had taken place the day before. Had we not been there the day before, we wouldn't have known a carnival had been there. Through the night a crew had worked tirelessly to make the place shine. We were ushered over by the 5K volunteers to a tent where we get our commemorative Under Armour T-shirt, water bottle, and participation medal. Surrounded again by Notre Dame faithful, we had the opportunity to strike up conversations with other runners. The 5K was more than just a run, it was an excuse to meet others and get out and try something new. It gave us an opportunity to socialize with people we otherwise wouldn't have met. That is truly what makes events like this special . . . the opportunities for new experiences in new places. I felt an energy I've never felt before a game. I was pumped and ready to be the best fan I could be. The adrenaline surging through my veins not only gave me a runner's high but also charged me up for a new day full of football, food, and friends. It was the Shamrock Series game day. What could be better?

Chapter 19
Mr. Time

A black circular clock hung on a stark white wall marking the 4:00 p.m. hour. I sat at my computer desk feverishly working. The keys on the laptop were warm from the overworked motherboard underneath. I had been working for hours, putting my MacBook to the test. We were both going strong and determined to finish the task at hand. Overheating and shutting down was not an option; we had deadlines.

I was producing a television special that needed to air that night at 6:00 p.m. It was a piece for the pregame broadcast of the NBA finals on TNT. Lebron James and the Cleveland Cavaliers were taking on Tim Duncan and the San Antonio Spurs for game three. The network kept calling me for updates. The interruptions actually slowed me down, but I was determined. "I will not miss this deadline," I said to myself as I worked away. The competitive nature of that particular project gave me the motivation to see it through. The clock turns to the 5:00 p.m. hour. Only sixty short minutes until my piece was scheduled to air. Somehow I had to figure out how to do three hours of work in thirty minutes. I turned off my office phone to minimize the distractions, buried my face in the computer, and kept pushing forward. Against all odds I kept going.

But being so immersed in my work, I forgot to turn my cell phone off and, of course, it rang. I looked down and saw the words "Dad Cell" on the iPhone screen. *Not now, Dad,* I thought to myself and kept going. The phone took the call to voicemail as I reengaged with what I was doing. The moment I got my full attention back to what I was doing, my cell rang again. It was Dad—again. He normally only calls back-to-back like that when there is an emergency. I looked at the clock. 5:30 p.m. now. I looked back at my phone, concerned that this might be a serious call. I answered.

"Hello, Mark," my dad said as he normally does. I can tell instantly by his lighthearted delivery that there was no emergency.

"What is it, Dad?" I asked. "I am really under the gun here."

He casually responded, "Well son, what are you doing?"

I can tell he doesn't pick up on the urgency in my voice, so I politely said, "Dad, I have to go. I'll call you later." He always moves at his own pace, and this time that pace felt more sluggish than normal.

He said, "Well before you go, I want to ask you a question."

"Yes, Dad?" I hastily replied.

"Do you want to go to the Navy/ND game this year? I think I can get tickets. I was talking to Howard and . . ." The clock now read 5:45 p.m. In my panic, I just hung up my phone. I felt bad about hanging up on my father like that, but I had no choice. The clock doesn't stop, and I was sure the network was going crazy since I had turned off my office phone. I was running out of time fast.

Oh that Mr. Time. He is my biggest rival. He is my worst enemy and my best friend. He brings out the best in me and then beats me up. He is relentless, testing me, pushing me, or trying to knock me out of the game. Look what he made me do. Because of him, I hung up on my father who was just trying to ask me about the Navy vs. Notre Dame game. Ironically, that's a classic football game that Mr. Time hasn't been able to put an end to.

Not every rivalry story is about who beat up who, or who knocked who out of the playoff hunt. Some go much deeper than that. Some have meaning beyond the game. Sometimes it is appropriate to look at the game of football as a window into bigger issues. One of the most honorable matchups in modern-day sports is between the Navy Midshipmen football team of the United States Naval Academy and the Notre Dame Fighting Irish. This particular game has a past unlike any other—not to mention that it has been played annually since 1927. That commitment makes it the longest uninterrupted rivalry in college football. As of this writing, Notre Dame leads the series 77–13–1. But the number of wins and losses is not the narrative that should be looked at when you talk about the game. It is more a story of honor, fortitude, and brother helping brother.

There is a reason Notre Dame and the navy unequivocally face off each year. The Irish and Midshipmen started the football tradition before the Great Depression, but that period of financial hardship wasn't what created the lasting bond between the two schools. The true intercollegiate friendship started later, around the time of World War II. So many of our nation's young men were going off to war. That effort affected many American institutions, but especially Notre Dame. At that time the university was still an all-male school, so attendance was dangerously low. It has been reported that the enrollment count was less than 3,000 at one point. Notre Dame, like many colleges, faced severe financial difficulties during World War II. Some believed, in fact, that the school would not survive the war. It needed help, desperately.

Enter the US Navy. Like a savior riding in on a white horse, or maybe more appropriately, on a battleship, the Navy made the grounds of Notre Dame a training center for V-12 candidates. It was basically an ROTC program that gave the Naval candidates access and use of the school facilities. In return for Notre Dame's hospitality, the US Navy paid the university enough to keep it afloat. Without the training program, the University of Notre Dame might not be here today.

Since World War II there has been an open invitation from the Irish to play the navy in football indefinitely. The Irish consider the annual game restitution on a debt of honor. There is a mutual respect between these two institutions—so much so that the series is called the "Friendly Rivalry." It has been over seventy years since the US Navy bailed out the Irish, yet I believe there is something we can learn still from the game—that there is no greater gift than a

121

helping hand. We were put on this earth to serve God and one another. The Notre Dame vs. Navy series is a great example of how sport can remind us of friendship and trust. When I watch this particular game, I don't think of the wins and losses. The series means more than that. I see a story of honor, respect, and helping those in need. A seemingly timeless series that should go on as long as decisions makers remain principled.

Something that wasn't timeless was my deadline for the TNT special. The last time I remembered looking at the clock was 5:50 p.m. I finished my assignment and hit the liberating "send" button. It was out of my hands and in full control of the Interweb. I didn't get a confirmation of receipt via email from the network, nor did they return my calls after I left multiple voicemails. I was in the dark. Literally and figuratively. (My building was shutting down for the day, and all the lights were going out.) There was a TV with cable in the kitchen, so I flipped it on and tuned in to TNT. Charles Barkley was on-cam, bashing Cleveland like he usually did at the time. Ernie Johnson interrupted the barrage and sent it over to Craig Sager, who was out on the street in Cleveland. He was giving his usual background piece on the city. As he delivered the narrative, he stood out in front of the Rock and Roll Hall of Fame. Now, interestingly enough, the Rock Hall sits on Lake Erie right next to the USS *Cod* Submarine Memorial. And wouldn't you know it, the old navy ship was lit up beautifully and could clearly be seen in the shot.

It reminded me to call my dad back on the phone. I dialed him up, and he answered on the first ring. "You watching the pregame?" I asked.

"I sure am. So why are you working so late?" he responded.

I began to answer, "Well Dad, I was working on a piece that was supposed to air tonight, but I think I missed my deadline." As soon as those words came out of my mouth, I heard a familiar sound on the TV. It was the intro to my piece. The network was running it. *Thank God*, I thought. *They got it in time.* I was still on the phone with my dad, so we got to watch it together. After it was over, I told my dad the whole story and why I had to hang up on him. I will never forget his response. After he heard my full apology he just said, "So about those Navy tickets . . ."

Thank You
to all United States
Armed Forces
men and women

Chapter 20
Confessions

D on't we owe it to ourselves to enjoy the happy times in life? Shouldn't we take a moment and let that joy sink in and appreciate what life has presented to us? After all, those moments are fleeting, and if we can't enjoy them, why are we even here?

That's the kind of moment I was having as I was sitting in a beer garden with my father, Big Al, Bobby, and Howard, celebrating an Irish victory. Notre Dame had defeated the Miami RedHawks earlier that day, 52–17. A blowout win. During halftime of that game, legendary coach Ara Parseghian was honored and a commemorative tribute film was played on the new jumbotron in the stadium. The tribute was apropos, considering Ara's coaching career started at the University of Miami (Ohio) in the 1950s.

Ara once said, "A good coach will make his players see what they can be rather than what they are." I feel the same way about parents. After all, parents are coaches too. They teach, guide, and set examples for their children. I guess you could say an engaged parent is a life coach, bringing up their children from infancy to childhood to adolescence and finally adulthood, always tailoring lessons and advice along the way to satisy the present moment. At least that is how I look at my parents. I am lucky to have them in my life. Their wisdom amazes me. I feel like I learn something new every time I sit and chat with them. Our post-game celebration in the beer garden after the Notre Dame victory over Miami was one of those chats with my father.

We sat in the back of the Evil Czech Brewery & Public House and just soaked up the joy of the Irish victory. We chatted about the game, Coach Parseghian's halftime tribute, and what our expectations were for the game the following week—just the basic ND banter. The server came over to our table with a new beer menu. The seasonal brews were just tapped and new varieties were just waiting to be consumed. When there are so many beer options, I can never choose just one, so I went with a flight. The server helped me pick samples of the five best on the list. Bobby did the same. Even though we were in a beer garden with fresh local brews, my father ordered a coffee, like he always does. It is rare to see him drink a beer, plus he was driving. The flights came to the table with an order of German-style pretzels. All was right in the world.

I tend to get a little chatty after a beer or two, and that day was no different. With the added fuel of an Irish win, I was having a good time. In the midst of our conversation, I asked my father a question about his younger years. I wasn't expecting much of an answer; my father never really talked about his youth too much. But for some reason, this time was different. To my surprise, he started telling stories I'd never heard before. His exploits as a teenager, how he met my mother, getting into trouble, and other colorful adventures I dare not recount.

I just sat back and listened in amazement. I had gone my entire life not knowing this stuff. How was that possible? *Why now?* I thought. The onset of anecdotes wasn't fueled by the beer. After all, my father had only been drinking coffee. Maybe it was the effect of an Irish victory coupled with the company of good friends—I don't know. But my father divulged narratives that made me see him in a new light—as a real person.

I think as children (and even sometimes as adults) we don't see our parents as real people. They are protectors, disciplinarians, and watchers put on this earth solely to guide us through life. At that moment I was able to see past all that and look at my father as a real human being with his own hopes and dreams. I thought, *Wow, hopefully my children will see me that way too someday.* After my wife and I raise them to be honest, self-sufficient, productive adults, of course.

One story from that night that sticks out to me was when my father talked about his early work life. He started in the steel mills right out of high school. A lot of people did that at the time in that part of the world. Most went that route because they had no other options. Not my father, though—he is a smart guy and could have done a lot of things. After all, he went to college for accounting, a far-removed discipline from manual labor. He made a conscious decision to forgo the accounting world and set his sights on the steel industry. He loved it. I don't know why. Filthy, hot, backbreaking work is not for me, but to each his own, right? As my dad was talking about his initiation into the brutal industrial landscape he disclosed details that were new to me. I always just thought that he loved the manual work, but it just so happens he was thinking of the bigger picture. He had a plan, a vision of what his adult life would be. At the time, pension plans were still very strong in the steel industry. Most men and women could cash out and retire after thirty years. That is what was so intriguing to my dad. He wanted to retire early in life and enjoy more free time. Big thoughts for an eighteen-year-old right out of high school. He figured that if he started as early as he could, then he could get in the thirty years and retire before the age of fifty. The idea was beautiful, and it worked . . . for the first twenty years, that is. He was two-thirds of the way to his goal when the bottom fell out of the industry, mills closed, and people lost their pensions. Life threw him a wicked curve ball. He was about forty years old with five children and had to start all over again. But he picked himself up, brushed off the soot, and kept moving forward.

I never realized he had a thought-out career plan so early in life. It made me think more of what my own plan is and what the backup to that plan should be. It also made me realize that life doesn't care about your plan. Things can change at the drop of the hat, and you need to be willing to roll with the punches. Now, my father never came out and said, "Mark, you need to have a plan." He just told his stories in regular conversation, but the message was clear.

It is astonishing the things we learn from parents. Even when they don't know they are teaching. While sitting at that table listening to my father I learned something new. Something I could apply to my own life. He was being completely honest in his articulations. I appreciated the moment because there is something really special about passing stories down to the next generation. It's like securing a part of yourself to live on in the future. I started the evening soaking in the joy of an ND win but finished with a sense of gratitude for my father's honesty. I decided in that moment that I wanted to be more open and transparent with people around me. I knew it might be difficult to do, but I realized the benefit of disclosing my thoughts and feelings more. I decided I was going to be the kind of parent that answers my children's questions with honesty and clarity. No matter how hard the questions may be. There is such freedom in honesty.

We packed up and hit the road for home the following day. As soon as I pulled into the driveway, my two little girls came running out to meet me. I scooped them up in my arms and gave them a huge hug. I was extra happy this time to see them. My oldest daughter asked me how the trip went. I said, "Go inside and grab your coats, I will tell you all about the trip over ice cream." Spending time with my father makes me realize how lucky I am to have parents as role models. It makes me appreciate the position in life I was born into. Not everyone has great parents, and I was blessed with two. That time with my father inspires me to be the best dad I can, to always be there for my children, and to always love them. When I returned home that day, I couldn't wait to talk to them, to tell them all about what happened in my life the past few days. I was excited to tell them stories that would help them better understand who I was on the inside, just like my father told me the night before. You can spend every day with a person, and if you open and share your thoughts, you can always learn something new.

Chapter 21
Amassing Motivational Memorabilia

K nowing when to hold on and knowing when to let go is something we all struggle with. Sometimes we make it out to be a colossal decision with immense pressure. Other times the decision is crazy easy. We never know until we are in that moment. Some people struggle with letting go of the possessions in their life. They hold on to them forever, refusing to move on. This chapter is all about the "things" I have collected over the years that spark specific significant memories. Believe me, I am not a hoarder. I'm the complete opposite actually. I don't like holding on to "stuff," but there are a few things I just can't let go of because they represent something special to me. These things spark memories, serve as reminders of important life lessons, or just make me happy. They are "things" that move me forward rather than hold me back.

❀❀❀

Being a Cleveland Browns fan is like being in a perpetual state of convalescence, annoyingly licking the wounds of weekly Sunday beatdowns. I had hoped all that would change on April 28, 2007. That was the day of the NFL draft—the Super Bowl for the Browns nation. It's the time of the year we all look forward to. It's when the Browns are actually on top. Usually they have high draft picks, which, in theory, means better player selection. That year (and almost every year) the Browns needed a quarterback, and there was one on top of the board that would bring excitement to the team. It was Brady Quinn. Now Brady excelled at the collegiate level, but the NFL is a totally different beast. Many things can go wrong, and players don't always work out, as we all have witnessed. But the draft is a time of hopeful optimism. It's a time when the focus shifts to potential and thoughts of "What if?" start to take root.

I was overjoyed when the Browns selected Brady late in the first round. Finally, a quarterback I could support. Whether he succeeded right away or had struggles early on didn't matter to me. He was a Golden Domer and had my support either way. Now, I don't buy Browns jerseys—ever. The team turns over too often, and it is rare for a successful player to stick around. Buying a jersey is like buying a new car in my opinion. They are really expensive and start to lose value the moment you take them off the lot. You may be able to wear a jersey for a few games, but usually something happens and that player is no longer on the team. The jersey gets outdated, or worse yet, you just get too embarrassed to wear it. This time was different though. It has been a while since a high-level Irish player was drafted by the Browns, so I was buying that jersey. I had extremely high hopes that I would wear this jersey on Sundays for many years. I envisioned it would get worn out from all the jumping and celebrating, spilled victory beer and nacho cheese dip. Sadly, I was wrong. In fact, I only wore that jersey to one game, and it was a loss. Lesson learned: Never buy a Browns jersey. Even if that player is a Domer.

I did keep the jersey though. It sits folded at the bottom of a dresser drawer. I don't see it very often, but when I do, I am reminded to take the good with the bad. It makes me think about how I set my expectations. I read somewhere that happiness directly corresponds to achieving an expected outcome. So if expectations are set high and not reached, then a feeling of failure is inevitable. But if expectations are set moderately and surpassed, a sense of achievement and happiness is likely. I guess what I take from all this is that it's better to set reasonable expectations and judge the outcome of events on a moderate scale. I'd rather feel excited than let down. So, you can imagine where I set the bar when I think about the Browns. Sorry, Cleveland.

✸✸✸

When someone refers to "the man in the yellow hat" what do you think of? Curious George, right? Most people do. In fact, I would venture to say almost everyone has some kind of childhood memory of those stories. They are a true literary classic. I remember my mother reading me those books before I went to bed. They entertained us and taught us important childhood lessons. As an adult, though, when I hear the phrase "the man in the yellow hat," I think of something completely different. I think of a gift I got from my in-laws. It is a yellow baseball hat with a blue ND logo on the front. But this is no ordinary hat; this one is special. On the brim of the hat there is a signature, written in black felt marker, of a very extraordinary figure. The signature reads "Lou Holtz." It's a real collector's item, and I display it on a shelf in my office for all to see.

I don't hold on to many things. In fact, clutter makes me feel uneasy. I find throwing things away oddly satisfying. I feel comfortable with clean, simple, and organized environments, free of extra junk. But this hat is not junk. It is a prized possession that I display proudly. I don't know Lou personally—in fact, I never even met the man before. But I have tremendous respect for him. He was a great football coach, yes, but he was an even better leader, speaker, and influencer. He is constantly infusing the world with antidotes to complacency, inspiring tales, and motivational words of wisdom. He is a very intelligent man with a gift for seeing the positive in this world and articulating his observations.

Something he once said in a graduation speech had a profound impact on how I view the world. He said:

> Life doesn't have to be complicated. I like to keep life simple. Do you realize there are only seven colors of the rainbow? Only seven. Look what Michelangelo did with

those seven colors. There's only seven musical notes. Look what Beethoven did with those seven notes. There's only ten numbers. Look what Bernie Madoff did with those ten numbers. The point I make is life doesn't have to be complicated. Say you need four things in your life. If you don't have any of these four things in your life, you're going to have a tremendous void. See, everybody needs something to do. Number two, everybody needs someone to love. Number three, everybody needs someone to believe in. In my case it's Jesus Christ, our Lord and Savior. But the fourth thing you need in your life is you need something to hope for.[1]

When I heard this for the first time, I was in awe. It's so simple and so true, and you'd think most of us would know this intuitively. But it's so powerful and reaffirming to hear someone else say it out loud. Hearing it reminds us that we all have more in common than we think. Human beings are meant to be happy, and we are all constantly in pursuit of that happiness. I can never judge a person for doing what makes them happy, no matter what it is. That is human nature. The yellow hat that sits on the shelf in my office reminds me of that. It has become a symbol to me to always do my best, keep trying, never be complacent, and always pursue happiness.

I put the hat on only one time. I put it on my head, looked in the mirror, and envisioned the man I wanted to be. That man is always pushing forward, he is always looking at the brighter side of life, and he is always dreaming. He has the four things in life that Coach Holtz talked about. He is rooted in faith and love. He is the image of what I strive to be. Of course, I will never get there 100 percent, that is the nature of life. But I will never give up trying. I took the hat off and put it back on the shelf. I will never wear it again. See, the man in the yellow hat is me—or at least the man I aim to be. It is a version of me that is holistically centered, fulfilled, and at peace with the world. I know I will never catch this man, but that won't stop me from trying.

✳✳✳

In my lifetime, the glory years for the Irish stretched from the mid-eighties to the mid-nineties. During that time, they went to nine New Year's Six bowl games. It was an exciting time to be a fan. Even the off-season was fun. During the spring games, the administration let their guard down and allowed fans access to players before the games. I remember running out onto the field in glorious fashion as a kid. The players would station themselves strategically across the field to meet fans and sign autographs. Naturally people gravitated toward the polarizing players at the time, like Rick Meyer, Ricky Watters, and Jerome Bettis, just to name a few. It was almost impossible to get their autographs on the field. Like bees to sugar, people swarmed these guys. I can see why the university stopped this endeavor with the security climate being what it is today. At the time, though, they encouraged it. Outside the stadium they would sell small 8 x 5-inch programs for the game. These were the big things at the time. From year to year we would collect them and hold on to them like trophies. Inside the program was the roster, player stats, and local ads. But our attention was always focused on something else in those programs. The top players of the year all had a full page to themselves. An action shot was printed with their name and number. The pages were designed specifically to get autographs. It became a badge of honor if you could collect the autographs of all the featured players. I was never able to. I came close a few times but never did it.

One year I decided to change my strategy. I went with quality over quantity. That year Jerome Bettis was the premiere player in college football. His popularity was as huge as his stature. He was a tailback that was built like a nose tackle. He was a remarkable specimen of humanity, a true once-in-a-generation talent. I remember making up my mind before the game to not give up until I had that autograph, even if it was the only signature I got. I disclosed my plan to my older sister, who preceded to tell me that it was a bad idea. "Don't waste your time," she said. "You'll never get that autograph. It's too hard." In fact, everyone else in our group had the same advice for me. But in true contrarian spirit, I decided to go against the group and get that autograph.

Right before the players came out of the tunnel, we made our way down to the gate that led onto the field. The security guards wouldn't let anyone onto the field until all the players got to their respective spots. So as you can imagine, there was plenty of pushing and shoving at the front of the line. Kids would throw elbows, step on toes, do just about anything to get an early advantage. I am not proud of it, but I did the same to secure my place in the front of the line. You had to. No pain no gain, as they say.

The players started to enter the field, I kept a close eye out for Mr. Bettis. I waited and waited behind that medal guard rail that was holding all us fans back as each player came out onto the field. I used that time to plan my path and strategize the quick jump I needed to get out in front of the crowd to reach Jerome first. It felt like an eternity up there. To my disappointment, Jerome never came out. The security guard announced he was about to open the gate and needed everyone to step back. "Wait!" I yelled. "Jerome isn't on the field yet!"

"I guess he ain't coming, kid," the security guard replied.

I was heartbroken, and my world shattered in that moment. All my planning and torment for nothing. Right when all hope was lost, I heard a voice yell, "There he is!"

I looked up and couldn't believe my eyes. It was him. He ran out onto the field with a white towel on his head for some reason. But there was no hiding from these fans. Everyone knew number six, "The Bus." The gate opened and out we ran like a stampede of wildebeest. With an adrenaline-fueled charge, it was every man for himself. Everything after that is a blur to me, a haze of green grass, thrown elbows, and herds of aggressively moving people. I do remember the moment the dust settled though. The coaches blew the whistle, and all the players ran back to the locker room to get ready for the game. The security guards feverishly ushered everyone off the field. I stood there for a moment, powerless to move. I reflected on what had just happened but everything was foggy. I thought, *Did I get hit in the head? Did I pass out?* I was so confused.

"Hey kid, get off the field!" a security guard yelled at me, snapping me out of my post-rumble trance. I still had my program in my hand. I opened it up to page twelve, Jerome's page. And what happened next I can only describe as pure bliss. In black felt pen writing, I saw the words "Go get 'em little man, Bus #6." I did it. I couldn't believe that had really just happened. I knew then what it felt like to earn a hard-fought victory.

I learned a lesson that day as well. I learned that focus and perseverance pays off. I learned to follow my dreams no matter what other people say—to do what was in my heart and always try my hardest. Only good things will come from that kind of effort. I am not sure if the autograph itself has much value anymore, but what I went through that day to get it and what I learned about myself in the process is priceless.

As I contemplated that experience, I came to realize that it is much better to try and fail than to not even try at all. I learned to embrace the fear of failure and to use it as psychological fuel. Most of the time things might not go as intended, but what you learn from the experience is more important. No matter what, always, always, always at least try, because sometimes things do go as planned. Sure, I only got one autograph that day, but getting that solo signature led me to discover something far more profound—not to mention that I had the best time boasting to my older siblings. There is nothing quite like the feeling you get when you can prove doubters wrong.

***

There is much debate these days on how to reward achievement, and there is more controversy about what achievement actually is. For example, we always hear someone complaining about the "everybody gets a trophy" trend, referring to participation awards that are often distributed to youth sports teams at the end of the season. Whether the team is the best or the worst doesn't matter, everyone gets a "trophy." On one hand, people argue this encourages mediocrity and breeds entitlement. However, others say it rewards commitment and fortitude. I can say I am completely divided on the issue. I can see both arguments. To be fair, the only thing I can do is to draw on my own experiences and not try to speak for others.

I played sports all my life and got those disputatious prizes at the end of each season. Honestly, I remember which trophies had meaning and which ones were merely a formality. The ones earned for excellence I always held with higher regard, while the others just went in a drawer. Of all the trophies I got as a kid, the award I prize the most came later in life.

You may recall when I talked about the 5K run earlier in this book that took place during the Shamrock Series fan events in Indianapolis. Upon crossing the finish line of that race, everyone was given an Under Armour water bottle and a participation medal. Now I didn't have the best time in the group—very far from it actually. I would say I probably had one of the worst times compared to everyone else running. But sure as rain, I got that medal. The thing is, though, I wasn't running against everyone else. I was running against myself. That was the first time I ever participated in a 5K. I struggled even signing up because I wasn't confident I could finish. I didn't want to embarrass myself, and I had no idea what to expect since I had never participated in one before. With some encouragement from my brother and Bobby, I made the leap and gave it a shot. I am so happy I did too, because that race was my catalyst to participate in many more. Now I can't wait to sign up for these things. They have become events in my life I can look forward to. We all need those in our life, things that excite us. They help us face new challenges every day and look at the future through a positive lens.

I keep that medal hanging on a shelf in my room. It is a reminder to try new things and to challenge myself. Technically, at first glance, it is just a "participation trophy," but to me it is something different. I know I didn't earn it for being the best, or even being good for that matter. I earned it for challenging myself and following through. Not to argue in favor of everybody getting trophies, but I think it is wise to look at what trophies actually represent. Sometimes they can have a lasting impact that helps motivate us to be better versions of ourselves. When it comes to giving out trophies at the end of a youth sports season, each situation in unique and to deny a child the tools to surmount challenges is a shame. Sometimes a trophy can be a motivational tool and sometimes it can encourage complacency. I learned to look past the physical trophy and embrace what it represents.

I hope my children will learn when to look at those seasonal mementos as celebrations of excellence and when to look at them as psychological fuel to try harder. I don't think you can choose one side of the argument or the other without focusing on the true meaning of the trophy. I got that participation medal for crossing the finish line at the 5K. It was the same medal given to the person who came flying in at first place and the person who moseyed on in dead last. But the symbolism wasn't about first and last, it was about accomplishment, perseverance, and dedication. Those are all traits worth acknowledging, especially to one's self.

Chapter 22
United We Stand

Have you ever noticed that everyone is friends when a birthday cake comes out? Why is that? When you are at a party and the cake is ready to make its debut, we all drop what we are doing and gather around, united in song. We stare into those burning candles with high hopes while our voices all merge in a harmonious outward sign of peace and happiness. For the briefest of moments, we set aside all differences to partake in a classic tradition. It really is a magical thought to think that birthday cake can solve so many social problems.

One year, the day after my birthday, I was driving through the Metroparks on my way to work. I wasn't feeling too well after my somewhat irresponsible indulgence the day before. There is only so much cake and ice cream a human being can consume, and I had tried to test just how much. But I digress. I was listening to the *Mike & Mike* radio show like I normally do. One of the co-hosts of the show, Mike Golic, is a huge Notre Dame guy, both figuratively and literally. In fact, his sons played football for the Irish. That is why I listened to that show in the first place—there was always an Irish "homer" opinion.

That particular day was a special edition of the program. Not because it was the day after my birthday, but because it was the very last show. The two Mikes were parting ways to pursue their own individual endeavors, and the show was coming to an end. I have to admit that I was sad they decided to discontinue the broadcast. For eighteen years it was fun tuning in to a program that had a favorable bias toward the Irish.

As my attention drifted between my aching, overstuffed stomach and the radio program resonating from the truck speakers, an interesting guest was announced on the show. It was Bill Curry. Bill is a retired football coach and player. He played for legendary figures like Vince Lombardi and Don Shula. He is a worldly man, and his knowledge of the game—and life in general—is astonishing. When he came on, my attention was locked to the program. I had high hopes (the kind of hopes you get when you see a birthday cake) for what bombs of wisdom he would drop on listeners. I wasn't disappointed. He said:

> On Friday nights the community huddles. And people sit together that never sit together the rest of the week. When someone's son scores a touchdown, the most unlikely hugs occur. Those children that have been raised to hate each other by the sick folks in our culture, they get in the locker room, they get in the huddle and they learn to love each other. And that love and respect, regardless of the color of one's skin, regardless of religion, regardless of national origin, lasts the rest of your life. Football is the only sport where every player needs every teammate on every play just to survive. Well, the United States of America is structured similarly. We seem to have forgotten that fact. So football is a little more profound than a lot of people understand, and that's what people need to hear.[1]

Wow! I thought to myself. He had just summed up the single greatest thing about football in such a profound way. His comments made football out to be more than just a game. It is the great unifier, the common ground, the foundation on which to build social equality. How amazing is that? It made me reflect on my own playing days. The time I spent on the field and how the game yielded friendships for me I wouldn't have had any other way. I thought about all the lessons I learned from the coaches I had. Always do your best, never give up, work until you get it right, be honest, be fair, don't make excuses, trust the person next to you, be trustworthy to them, work as a group, work as equals . . . The list could go on and on.

All those lessons relate to the game of football as well as the game of life. Bill Curry's words reminded me of that. I only played ball through high school, but the lessons I learned in that short time would last a lifetime. I can only imagine what kind of knowledge could be gained by playing the sport at the next level. What other kind of wisdom do Notre Dame players absorb in the locker room and on the field, I wonder?

Most people look at the university as a prestigious educational institution. I believe that to be true, but I also think some of the most important life lessons are learned outside the classroom. It is my opinion that book smarts will only get you so far, and, at some point, character and intuitive thinking will lead the way. That is why the football program helps support the educational component of the university. The players are learning invaluable lessons about teamwork, hard work, and discovering what they are made of. Football is so much more than a revenue-generating enterprise for any university. It helps shape the character of those who go through the program. I think a lot of times, as fans, we forget these player are still students. They are still young men trying to find their place in this world. They are still growing and developing.

That is why great coaches are so important. They are the ones who spend the most time with student athletes, teaching them and guiding them. We can only hope as a society that they are teaching the players the right thing. I want to believe that those coaches are genuine, honest, and fair, and that they are instilling morals and ethics in their teams. That has been my experience with the game. I look back on my playing days and think of the coaches I had. Sure, they were very tough, very loud, and very aggressive. But it was always for our own good. It was always about making us better men as well as better players, and we learned a lot from them. We learned from both their words and actions. It is amazing how a simple quote

141

from a great leader can make you look at the world differently. I can only imagine the lessons learned behind closed doors with legendary coaches and leaders like Knute Rockne, Frank Leahy, Ara Parseghian, Dan Devine, and Lou Holtz.

As I get older, I find I still enjoy getting gifts on my birthday. But not physical gifts. Rather, I enjoy time with family, knowledge, and insight. I got one of the best gifts that day driving in my truck to work. Thank you, ESPN Radio. Thank you, *Mike & Mike*. And thank you, Bill Curry, for putting into words why we all have come to love the game of football so much. Thank you for the way you so poetically wrapped up the true meaning of the game in a short, idyllic bow. I guess you can say the game of football is like birthday cake. When you are around it, you can't help but feel unified, awestruck, and maybe a little hungry.

Afterword
Final Drive

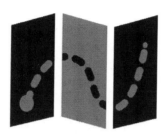

The University of Notre Dame, their football program in particular, has enriched my life in ways I can't even describe. And I wasn't even a student there. Whether you are totally for them or totally against them, you can't deny that Notre Dame is a very polarizing institution. Like coach Dan Devine said, "There are two kinds of people in the world, Notre Dame lovers and Notre Dame haters. And, quite frankly, they're both a pain in the ass."

I can agree with that. Notre Dame homers are committed diehards, and that loyalty transcends generations. My family is proof of that, and I know there are many others just like us. Notre Dame was—and is—a lifestyle for us. I am sure the "lovers" appreciate our commitment and the "haters" loathe it. I acknowledge that the fandom can get a little obnoxious (if not downright nauseating) to those who don't share the same passion, but it is that shared passion that brings my family closer together and the reason I cherish it so much. Yes, we love the Irish, but more importantly, we appreciate the bond it creates between us all.

For me, Notre Dame is an excuse to spend quality time with my father. Just as I couldn't wait for him to come home from work to play catch in the front yard when I was a kid, I can't wait for our trips to South Bend. As an adult, I don't spend as much time with my parents as I should—not with the hectic schedule of everyday life getting in the way. Trips to Notre Dame are a retreat from the rigors of the status quo. They provide the opportunity to allow those everyday troubles to fade away and return the focus to friends, family, and football.

I wrote these stories not only to commemorate my time spent with family but to also leave a legacy for my own children. I want them to know my father as I did; I want them to know how important these trips are for unifying us as a family; and I want to inspire them to keep this tradition alive. We don't have to go to South Bend, but I hope we will forever be present in each other's lives. As they grow older, I want them to know how important they are to me and their mother. I want them to know how much we love them. And I want them to understand how important family is to enriching our time on this earth. I hope the lessons I learned from my parents and the family traditions we forged will be passed down through the generations, creating stronger bonds and loyalties. You don't just build a church for Easter Sunday, after all. You build it to stand the test of time. Brick by brick, moment by moment, lesson by lesson the preverbal temple is built.

One of those bricks that resonates with me is something else coach Dan Devine said: "A team is a team is a team." I think this could also translate to "A family is a family is a family." *Family* is a word used to describe the people that are closest to you, and the world is a better place because of the moments we spend together. So, I send my deepest gratitude and appreciation to the University of Notre Dame in South Bend, Indiana, for being the Saint Peter of our family bonds—the rock from which we built our traditions.

Of all the ties that bind in this life, none are as deeply rooted as kinship. And nowhere else is that kinship more profoundly displayed in my family than when we're watching the Irish take the field on Saturday afternoons in fall. Those Saturday afternoons are precious to us, but nothing can last forever. I don't know when that final drive to South Bend will be, but I can tell you one thing: this family is ardently committed to each other and the Irish of Notre Dame.

When Coach Ara Parseghian was nearing the end of his tenure as the head ball coach he was asked, "After Notre Dame, what is there?" I think about what my answer to that question would be, and honestly, I don't have the slightest clue. But like Notre Dame, it will be something that brings out the best in us. It will be something that strengthens our relationships and something we can all be proud of. To that I say amen.

End Notes

Chapter 2
1. Murray A. Sherber, *Shake Down the Thunder: The Creation of Notre Dame Football* (Bloomington, IN: Indiana University Press, 2002), pp. 178–179.

Chapter 3
1. "Lake Dawson Discusses GM Opening," Panthers TV video, posted February 2, 2018, http://www.panthers.com/media-vault/videos/Watch-Lake-Dawson-discusses-GM-opening-/4a00b26e-05bd-42fb-9ce7-d05f1b0c569e.

Chapter 5
1. Andrea Adelson and Adam Rittenburg, "Reliving the Glory Days of the Notre Dame-Miami Rivalry," *ESPN*, November 10, 2017, http://www.espn.com/college-football/story/_/page/rivals111017/miami-hurricanes-notre-dame-fighting-irish-glory-days-rivalry.
2. Ibid.
3. Ibid.
4. Ibid.

Chapter 7
1. Arthur J. Hope, CSC, *Notre Dame—One Hundred Years* (Notre Dame, IN: University of Notre Dame Press, 1999), http://archives.nd.edu/hope/hope02.htm.

Chapter 8
1. Notre Dame University, "The Fighting Irish," *Traditions*, http://www.und.com/trads/nd-m-fb-name.html.

Chapter 14
1. Notre Dame Archives, "Notre Dame vs. Michigan," *Notre Dame History*, http://www.archives.nd.edu/about/news/?p=190.
2. John L. Duffy, ed.,"The Foot-Ball Trip," *The Chronicle*. 19, no. 1, December 3, 1887, p. 68.

https://books.google.com/books?id=vbfmAAAAMAAJ&printsec=fr
ontcover#v=onepage&q&f=false.
3. Notre Dame Archives.

Chapter 11
1. Rick Reilly, "Paint Like a Champion," *ESPN*, December 21, 2012,
http://www.espn.com/espn/story/_/id/8765862/notre-dame-play-
champion-today-sign.

Chapter 21
1. "Lou Holtz: Undergraduate Commencement Address 2015,"
YouTube video, 17:56, posted by Franciscan University of Steubenville
on May 13, 2015,
https://www.youtube.com/watch?v=M3LOo_Ccyws.

Chapter 22
1. "Former NFL player and Coach Bill Curry Shares Powerful Message
of Unity on ESPN," SportsSpectrum video, 1:58, posted by Jason
Romano on November 17, 2017,
https://sportsspectrum.com/sport/football/2017/11/17/former-nfl-
player-coach-bill-curry-shares-powerful-message-unity-espn/.

Acknowledgments

The Notre Dame crew throughout the years
Robert "Hurricane" Hamer (Dad)
Janet Hamer (Mom)
Rob Hamer
Laura (Hamer) Gardner
Katie (Hamer) Rottmayer
David Hamer
Howard "Howie" Lewis
Loretta Lewis
Stephanie (Lewis)
Melissa (Lewis)
Nina (Lewis)
Albert "Big Al" Dota
Eilene Dota
Robert "Bobby" Dota
Loyde Griffith
Zack Griffith
Jessica (Griffith) Loftus

Childhood friends who contributed to the journey
Nick Marsh
Jamie Kelley

Establishments that contributed to the experience
The Original Pancake House – South Bend, Indiana
Rocco's Restaurant – South Bend, Indiana
Doc Pierce's Restaurant - Mishawaka, Indiana
Evil Czech Brewery – Mishawaka, Indiana
St. Charles School and Church – Boardman, Ohio

Special Thanks

To my wonderful family. My beautiful wife, Sally, and my amazingly bright and enthusiastic little girls, Avery and Evelyn. You are a true godsend. I love you with all my heart, forever.

To my mother and father who shaped me into the man I am today. Through their unconditional love and mentorship I learned what it means to be a fair, honest, and dedicated father and husband. They are my heroes and inspire me to be the best person I can be.

The University of Notre Dame.

About the Author

Mark Andrew Hamer is an award-winning film director, editor, and writer. He has traveled the globe trying to quench his insatiable appetite for knowledge and inspirational stories. In his adventures he has climbed a mountain to study the remains of a twelfth-century castle in Germany, sat in a supersonic rocket car designed to go 1000mph in England, ate wild berries off a vine growing up a skyscraper in Brazil, and explored a decrepit power station in Wales that produces invisible steam hot enough to bisect anything that crosses its path. He has even spent a week marooned on a remote island in the Georgian Bay with no running water or power. He has been witness to many edifying situations in many extraordinary places around the world, but none as profound as those experienced closer to home in the American heartland.

As a child growing up in Youngstown, Ohio, Mark was groomed to be a Notre Dame football fan. He traveled to South Bend every year with his father to watch the Irish play. In Mark's opinion, it's life-changing family adventures that truly shape a person. And even though he was once seen consuming crab cakes with his fingers in the presence of a US president, he has become a more refined and better human being thanks in part to his experiences traveling with his father to South Bend.

Made in the USA
Middletown, DE
15 September 2018